BRAND THE WAY YOU THINK

BRAND THE WAY YOU THINK

MONETISE YOUR MIND AND BECOME THE
MUST-HAVE IN YOUR MARKET

SUZI GRAY

authors
AND CO.

First published in Great Britain in 2024
by Authors & Co.
www.authorsandco.pub

ISBN 978-1-915771-60-5 (paperback)

Graphics by Rachel Shillcock

CONTENTS

PREFACE

This is for the deep thinkers and feelers; the ones who have so much wisdom within they struggle to translate the essence of it; the ones who care about impact, integrity, intimacy, and who lead with love. This is for the ones who are secretly a little scared of their potential. The ones who are ready to escape the epidemic of generic, go to different depths, and truly own what everyone else can see makes them so special. This is for the ones who want to monetise their mind, articulate their wisdom with conviction, and become the must-have in their market – the ones who were born to be the irresistible authority.

This is for the ones who are ready to become The One.

1

INTRODUCTION

Your brain is a goldmine. The problem is that you don't know the best, strongest, most natural-for-you way to distil and translate what's inside it through your personal brand – a way that pulls the perfect people closer, like a loved one's warm and familiar embrace; a way that has the perfect people experiencing tiny transformations just by being in your presence; a way that has the perfect people saying, *"How can I work with you?"* before they've even heard what you offer. For you, knowing your stuff and being of service is the easy part, but communicating the extraordinary value of that, in a way that feels in integrity… Not so much. That's the real reason you aren't (or don't feel like) the irresistible authority yet. And that's where I hope this book will help.

Branding the way you think isn't about trying to shine brighter. You already shine like a diamond. It's about making sure you're shining in the right way, for the right people. You don't need to outshine the competition when you've made them irrelevant.

BUILD YOUR CASE, BUILD YOUR BRAND

"Not guilty."

I locked my eyes on the defendant as the verdict was read out. Her face cracked, blonde hair framing the relief written all over it. But I wasn't watching so closely because I shared her relief. It was because, deep in my gut, I believed she was guilty. My curiosity wanted to witness how it felt to know you'd got away with it, especially because I was part of the reason she was walking free.

She stood in the dock. I sat on the jury's bench. I'd spent the last few days hearing the cases made for and against this woman's guilt. Two sets of narratives meticulously crafted to try to persuade us one way, or the other. The prosecution wanted to make us believe she was guilty, the defence wanted to make us believe she wasn't. Each barrister presented a series of facts, evidence, and arguments to help shape our belief of the truth. Lawyers play in the grey. They knew our verdict would not be decided from one puzzle piece of the presentation but from the compound effect of seeing all the pieces together. They chose which pieces to present, and when and how to present them in order to strengthen their narrative and our belief in it.

In the end, it was a unanimous verdict. She walked free. You might be wondering why I voted not guilty when I believed the opposite. Put simply, the evidence presented to us wasn't strong enough to meet the standard required to find her guilty of the crime she was charged with. The law was the rulebook, whether we liked it or not.

But what happens when you get to make the rules? What happens when you get to set the standards for the decisions made? What happens when you get to make a case for yourself? As experts with a business and personal brand, that's exactly the position we're privileged enough to be in. All we need is the internet and our intellect and we can create a reality far beyond what we were ever told was possible in school. Every decision is our own:

- How we show up for an audience.
- What we package and offer them.
- How we articulate the value of our expertise.
- Who we work with.
- How we deliver results.
- The kind of experience we create for anyone who comes into contact with us.
- The way we lead ourselves and others.
- What we say yes to.
- What we say no to.
- The actions we take.
- The actions we don't take.

It sounds deliciously liberating. And it is. We have the kinds of opportunities those who came before us never did. But with liberation comes a new kind of fear. When we venture into the unknown without evidence that it's the "right" path, and realise we're our own leader, we don't just have the opportunity to change the rules, *we get to play an entirely different game*. For many, that's enough to cause them to turn back to what feels familiar. There's a level of safety that comes with the well-trodden path. Others choose to settle without even exploring the alternative, even if they know they're capable of more. Others don't even realise the opportunity is there for the taking. But you and I are different. We're made of grit and guts and uncommon courage. And now? We're too far gone. In many ways, we consider ourselves unemployable. The game we've decided to play and the opportunity we've accepted are too magnificent to give up on, even when it feels like our soul might buckle from the weight of the responsibility we've chosen to place upon it.

A few years after I'd sat on this jury, I attended an event where I randomly bumped into the defence barrister who had won the case (I was a practising employment lawyer at the time). Conversation flowed as smooth as the wine and, when I casually admitted I'd sat on one of his juries, he agreed the evidence against the defendant wasn't strong enough and that it was right *in the eyes of the law* that she had been acquitted. Read into that what you will. The truth didn't appear to win that day but as we all know, this is a world where the best *case* wins, and that's what personal branding is really about; building your own case. Being your own best advocate. Your brand should reflect your truth but that truth needs to serve a purpose. You're not just building a brand to get likes. You're crafting a narrative to change lives.

YOU GET TO CONTROL THE NARRATIVE

There were four coffins lined up in a row. I remember standing in a dress the colour of darkness thinking: *Coffins are made for bodies. Not human remains.* But remains were all we had. I'm almost surprised each time the 17th of July comes around again. In 2014, civilian plane MH17 was shot down by a Russian missile over a sunflower field in Ukraine. I lost my Uncle Andrew, Aunt Estella, and my two young cousins, Jasper and Friso, who were only 14 and 12 years old. They were headed from Amsterdam to Malaysia for a once-in-a-lifetime trip. Instead, they were part of a once-in-a-lifetime tragedy.

Two hundred and ninety-eight bodies fell from the sky that day. I became addicted to the news, watching my family's faces splashed across the TV on repeat, as if I was waiting for someone to say it was all a mistake. I tortured myself looking at images of the crash site on social media, wondering if I'd see something, someone, I knew. The most disturbing thing, though, was the journalists. They were hungry and our pain tasted good. They hounded my elderly grandmother. They persisted in knocking on our door, posting notes through the letterbox, and even tailing my mum's car while she drove to the supermarket. They sent me private messages asking if I could confirm I was a relative. Then, one of them said something I'll never forget: *"If you don't take control of the narrative, other people will do it for you."* That's when we decided it was time to write a family statement confirming they were all on the plane. It was our place to communicate the truth, not other people's place to assume it. As sad as this story is, it's exactly what happens every day in running a business as a personal brand. We're either controlling the narrative, or it's being assumed for us.

If you ask a room of people to define a brand, every single one will give you a different answer. At its core, a brand is a perception. It's what "they" whisper to their friends when you're not listening. Their perception is your reputation. You might be thinking that means branding is outside your control but there lies your opportunity because if you're fiercely intentional about the way you build your brand, *you can shape the perception for them.* Actual value is not the same as perceived value. It's not your expertise that will drive your perceived value; it's your brand. Your job is to focus on what you *can* control and surrender to what you can't. When you do, you'll craft a brand narrative that gets you seen, heard, respected, and paid by the right people. Within that narrative, you have:

1. An identity – this is primarily made up of personality traits, personal philosophies, and industry perspectives.
2. An audience – this includes a particular group of people you're seeking to connect with and (in some cases) provide a product or service to in exchange for money.
3. A mission – to help that particular group of people experience some kind of transformation using a particular set of skills.
4. A challenge – to show those people why they should choose you and continue to choose you over others who claim to be able to solve their problems or fulfil their unmet needs.

You communicate that narrative through your presence. It's the strength of your narrative and the power of your presence that will define the success of your brand and whether somebody believes you are the person to invest time, money, and energy in… or not. You might feel like you've given your audience everything they need to make the decision you want them to make, and then they go hire somebody else. That doesn't mean you're not the right person; it means you need to work on how to communicate that you are. Stellar reputations don't exist by default, they exist by design.

Branding is a vast, layered topic. The main focus of my work is branding the way you *think* – how your unique wisdom translates in a way that's relevant and resonant to the right people, the people you're perfectly poised to help. It's not about fancy words, shiny marketing, or trendy tactics. As an expertise-based business owner, when you're grounded in your thought leadership and master the energetic art of communicating your perspectives in a strategic way, you're well on your way to positioning yourself as – and actually *being* – the irresistible authority. And authority is where you find recognition, reputation, and reward.

"*JUST BE YOURSELF*": MISLEADING PERSONAL BRANDING ADVICE

I'll bet the millions I don't have yet that you've been told this so many times on your entrepreneurial journey – including by people who wouldn't *dare* show up on Instagram without a face filter – that you've started to believe it's true. And that's the reason you're not one of those overnight success stories yet, even though you know the real success stories actually take years. If only you could just be yourself online, *then* you'd have a competitive edge so sharp it makes you dangerous. *Then* you'd "unlock a new level" of authority that makes other experts look like amateurs. *Then* you'd have so many potential clients knocking on your virtual door, oohing and ahhing over your offers, that you'd actually have to start saying no.

The premise is pure: Get paid for being exactly who you are, ideally doing something you get a thrill from and are brilliant at. No more putting on appearances. No more dialling down the personality you were born with. No more buttoning up your self-expression so it's palatable to all. Don't get me wrong, I'm 100% on board with that premise. There are so many opportunities available for us now, opportunities that our ancestors would have wept over and then leapt at like wolves. We have the internet, which is accessible even from 10,000 feet in the air. We have social media, which (for the most part) is free. We have infrastructure that supports face-to-face relationships. We have a viciously overwhelming amount of information about anything and everything literally at our fingertips. And we have our brains, hearts, and independence. There is no shortage of opportunity, but there's an ocean of people wondering *how* to simply "be themselves" in a competitive online space and get paid for it.

The problem is threefold.

Firstly, we've grown up being told by various people in various ways that who we are *is not enough*. Therefore, showing up as we truly are, bearing our flaws to be judged by an audience short on time, overwhelmed with distractions, and sometimes, lacking the ability to think critically, feels like a risk. If we weren't enough for the people we were closest to, why would we be seen as enough by strangers? What happens if you show up as "all" of yourself, and then people don't buy from you? Or you're disappointed by the reaction? What will you make that mean?

Secondly, we still have to craft the narrative. The dark side of the belief that personal branding means just being yourself is that you feel an obligation to show the world everything. Just like your social media channels aren't meant to be robotic and absent of personality, they're not meant to be your personal diary either. You don't develop a reputation as an irresistible authority for just being yourself and showing your personality. That really *isn't* enough. How does your unique skillset and way of thinking solve a problem? Your presence still has to serve an ultimate purpose. People won't pay for access to your wisdom because it's available, they'll do it because it's relevant to them. You don't become known for who you are; you become known for your perspectives, ideas, stories, and results. This is driven not by a niche, but by a narrative.

Thirdly, it's all too easy to tie our identity to our expertise, results, and business as a whole. When our worth is wrapped up in our business, it's a slippery slope. As a personal brand, if being yourself equates to whether you get paid or not, and you haven't reached the kind of success you desire (yet), it can make you think you need to become someone else. When *you* are what people are buying, there's always pressure to be the person you think they want you to be, and that can take you further away from who you truly are. This is the fastest way to build a brand and business that either burns you out or that you want to burn down. Or, if things go really badly, both.

There's a subtle shift to make here. The goal is not necessarily to get paid to be yourself, it's not to get paid for being someone you're not. Your sense of self must be separate from people's perception of you. Your personal brand is based on you, but it's not *who you are*. It's an extension of you. Your presence is something you cultivate without being insincere. The truth is, it's not hard to be yourself when you've unbecome everything you never were in the first place. That's the real challenge. Once you remove the layers of expectations, "shoulds", and attempts to prove your worth, you're left with the truest expression of you. And only when you're grounded in that can you become your best competitive advantage. Personal branding is your opportunity to turn up the volume on the parts of yourself that are relevant and resonant. That's when you become captivating for the right reasons. You don't have to bring all of yourself to the table if you don't want to. You don't have to be someone you're not. You just need to be intentional about what you've got.

THE PROBLEM WITH FOCUSING ON RESULTS

The traditional way of marketing places all the importance on specific, tangible, external results. Do this and you will make x amount of money/lose x amount of weight/meet your soulmate, etc., often supported by social proof that makes it sound deliciously easy. This gets people to buy, of course, but it also creates three problems.

1. Results Entitlement

When the process of transformation is reduced to a sentence or two in that way, it can make people believe the transformation is guaranteed. This then makes them think they don't have to put much effort in, they don't really have to work for the result, and that they're entitled to the transformation simply by investing in the process, which, of course, is not the case at all.

2. Value Dilution

Marketing in this way places all the value on achieving the final result rather than the often "un-articulatable", intangible, internal shifts that are actually the creators of the final result. The marketing dilutes the value of the exact place where the growth occurs. This links to Point One. People don't realise the depth of internal work required to achieve an external result because that wouldn't sell so well.

3. Worth Attachment

People end up tying their internal worth to an external result. If all the focus and value is placed on that result, how could they not? And then, if they don't achieve it, instead of seeing how far they've come, they see how far they didn't go. Then they make it mean that something is wrong with them, something they have to buy another "simple solution" to fix.

These issues are all a result of marketing being too focused on outcomes and not enough on what it takes to get them. If the transformation your work facilitates is difficult to attach a specific, tangible, external result to, and is difficult to condense into one or two sentences, you're not doing marketing wrong. You don't have to make wild promises to sell more or to attract buyers who are more advanced in their journey. Instead, build and brand a body of work that shows how you can uniquely support someone through their transformation. What do they need to bring to the table for you to do that effectively? Where does the magic really happen? What discomfort can they expect there, and how will you be there for them? How do you want them to see themselves as they embark on their next chapter? This is what will actually attract people who are looking for a partner on their level, not a guru on a pedestal.

KNOWLEDGE VERSUS WISDOM

Knowledge is not the same as wisdom, which is why being an expert is not the same as being an authority. It's not about the knowledge you have, it's about the way that knowledge manifests through you. Knowledge is what you know;

wisdom is how you use it. An expert knows the answers; an authority asks the right questions. You can be the smartest person in the room, but that doesn't make you wise.

Tilly Smith was only ten years old. It was Boxing Day 2004, and she was taking a leisurely morning stroll with her parents along Mai Khao Beach, Thailand. The sea was frothy, and Tilly noticed the water wasn't going in and out like it normally would. It reminded her of something she'd learned in geography class only a couple of weeks prior. She announced to her parents that a tsunami was coming. Her parents didn't believe her, after all, she was only a kid, so what could she know? There were no waves on the horizon. But Tilly persisted, getting more distressed, and told her parents she was leaving the beach, begging them to do the same. At this point, her father said to a security guard, *"Look, you probably think I'm absolutely bonkers, but my daughter's completely convinced there's going to be a tsunami."* The whole beach was evacuated, and just as people piled into the second storey of a nearby hotel, a thirty-foot wave slammed the shore. 227,898 people died in the 2004 Indian Ocean earthquake and tsunami. Mai Khao Beach was one of the few beaches in Thailand with no reported casualties. Tilly saved around a hundred lives that day, all because she was wise enough to apply her knowledge and brave enough to use her voice.

As a personal brand and thought leader, your brain is your biggest asset. You don't sell physical property (things you can touch and hold in your hands), you sell intellectual property. But this goes much further than knowledge. Intellectual property is not what you know, it's the way you *think* about what you know. It's your unique perspectives, ideas, and interpretations of your industry. This distinction is important.

Knowledge gives you a foundation but wisdom is how you can be an original in a noisy world. If you want to monetise your expertise through thought leadership, master communicating the context of it. The expertise itself won't position you as an authority. Demonstrating the way you think, in a way that's *relevant* and *resonant*, will.

Your worth is not defined by how much of an expert you are. Knowledge may look good on paper, but it's wisdom that will position you as an authority. In school, I was smart on paper, but in life, I knew diddly squat, which is normal because I was a teenager. It's only with time and putting myself in particular situations that I've grown in self-awareness and become wiser. I've learned that wisdom is not just about the mind but also about the body and soul. It's about intuition, discernment, and deep self-trust. As soon as you allow someone else's advice to override what your inner voice is screaming at you in silence, you hand your power over to them. You give them the reins to your life. It's a *Sliding Doors* moment. Listen to yourself and life plays out this way; listen to them and life goes in a different direction, one that can be difficult to come back from. There's no right or wrong way, there's just a choice. Part of our job as humans is to sit in the unknowing without mentally melting.

BRAND WHAT YOU DO VERSUS BRAND THE WAY YOU THINK

When I was in a frenzy of postpartum hormones, waking in the twilight hours to pop my newborn baby on the boob, I'd occasionally scroll on social media and see ads related to baby anything-and-everything. One particular ad I saw time and again was about sleep, and how both me and my baby could get more of it if I joined their paid membership. I did join, even though our sleep was pretty good at that point. Well, this quickly sucked all the joy out of my parenting experience. The membership recommended a schedule for napping, feeding, and playing with your baby, based on their age, and I realised this approach was a gentle introduction to sleep training, which was not something I wanted to do. While I was interested in the result offered, I wasn't interested in the pathway to get it (to be clear, I don't judge parents who make the decision to sleep train their children, though I do wish there was more information available on what normal baby sleep actually looks like and support *that*). For me, it was more that the result promised wasn't worth the effort. It wasn't just about a result. It was about how I got the result.

What does branding the way you think actually mean? Let's imagine two people are baby sleep experts. Both provide advice and support on baby sleep. Both have qualifications of some kind that suggest they know what they're talking about. Both are focused on helping your infant sleep better at night. Their promise might be: *"I'll show you how to get your little one to sleep 10-12 hours at night."* Both have testimonials that support this promise. This is an example of branding what they do. The focus is on the expertise and the result.

There are two major issues here. The first relates to the potential buyers. For some potential buyers, expertise and results are enough to get them to hand over their money. These buyers fall on the more desperate end of the spectrum (which is how many parents of newborns feel!). All they're interested in is the result, and as long as they believe a person can get them a result, they don't care how it manifests itself. But what about buyers like me? Ones who do care about the "how"?

We want to see who you are and how you think before feeling good about our decision.

The second issue is the competition. This example speaks of two people in the same industry/niche. But what if there are a hundred? A thousand? All selling the same result? There has to be a reason to choose *you* – and you never want it to be because you were the cheaper option. This is where positioning plays its part, along with using your perspectives to drive perception.

When you build a brand around what you do, there will always be competition, but when you build a brand around the way you think, competition becomes irrelevant.

THE EVOLUTION OF A THOUGHT LEADER

As humans, we constantly evolve. Our thinking, expression, clients, offers, and therefore, our personal brands, constantly evolve, too. We can choose to evolve in private, or we can choose to be witnessed in it. If you choose the latter, you're already on your way to becoming a thought leader. A thought leader contributes new ideas to their industry. They could be dangerously disruptive or beautifully simple.

The most difficult part of writing this book is knowing that my thoughts will have evolved beyond the ink by the time it's published. It would have been easy for me to have waited and waited until my ideas had been incubated long enough to be "worthy" of eternalising in a book, but that's the trap right there. When we see our future thinking as infinitely more worthy than our current thinking, our current thoughts won't see the light of day… Which means they won't reach the people they can help *right now*… Which means our work doesn't have the ripple effect we want it to... Which means we don't create the legacy we long for. The key is not having the ideas but sharing them. It sounds obvious, and yet this is exactly where people get tied in knots and succumb to what I call the epidemic of generic. They don't trust in the power of their unique perspective, so they dilute it to blend in. Or they worry that if it hasn't already been shared then it must be a bad idea, so they hoard it. Or they think the ideas they contribute have to be revolutionary and that feels too intimidating, so they stay in an echo chamber.

The type of thought leader I'm referring to in this book is a thought leader with something to sell. Your personal brand is a means to an end. You're not spreading ideas for the sake of it, or for free. You're not giving your opinion simply to oppose another. You're sharing unique perspectives with the deliberate intent of creating tiny transformations within a particular group of people. That's how impact begins. The compound effect of those tiny transformations is what you're really selling. If you consider yourself a business owner and you *don't* consider yourself a thought leader (or don't see yourself becoming one), I'd urge you to rethink, because if all you're building a brand around is what you do, you're commoditising yourself and doing your wisdom a disservice. If you want to build true brand authority, there comes a point when you have to be known for more than what you do. You have to build a brand around the way you think. You don't have to want to speak on stage, write books, or be globally recognised to be a thought leader. You can simply have powerful perspectives you want to share with the world so people can 1) think and act in new ways and, 2) know you're the right one to help them fulfil an unmet need.

If you want to be "just" a service provider, that's fine! But if your ambitions burn bigger, and you want to become known for something; if you want to build your credibility, authority, and a reputation that goes beyond your client results; if you want to shift your business model or diversify your offerings; if you want to position yourself in a more sophisticated way; if you want visibility opportunities that make your soul squeal with delight… it's not enough to be great at what you do. Just because you build it doesn't mean they will come. You need to step into your thought leadership and show the world why you're The One. We have already entered the era of the thought leader. Gone are the days when you could sell pretty much anything online without doing very much. Now attention spans are shorter, competition is fiercer, and buyers are more discerning. A thought leader is someone who transforms others by sharing their ideas, insights, stories, and perspectives rather than just telling them what to do. It's a more evolved and embodied way of teaching. You're already incredible at what you do. Now it's time to show the world how you think.

HOW TO USE THIS BOOK

This is less of a "how to do" book and more of a "how to think" book. Stronger thinking will always lead to stronger doing. Thinking too much and doing too little means slow and hindered progress. Thinking too little and doing too much means fast progress in what may be the wrong direction. Thinking in a vacuum means you may miss the magic. There's no right or wrong. Only lessons. You can think your way to greatness, you can act your way to greatness. Ideally, we want to choreograph a dance between the two. Shall we begin?

2

THE FOUR AUTHORITY PROFILES

After working with business owners with personal brands since 2012, I've been able to broadly categorise people into four authority profiles based on the way they think: the Hidden Gem, the Messy Mover, the Lost Rebel, and the Irresistible Authority. This is a starting point for deciphering why you're not in a category of one already (or you are, but it doesn't feel like home).

Let me give you some context. I used to call myself a professional clock-watcher. Not just because my job as a lawyer didn't fulfil me in the way I needed a job to, but because my job was *literally to watch the clock.* My firm used to bill in six-minute increments (which meant I had to track my time in six-minute increments – possibly the worst part of the job!). One of my litigation superiors pointed out one day that most of his billable hours were not spent doing anything, they were spent *thinking*. In other words, we got paid to think. Our compounded knowledge, experience, skillset, and the natural way our brains operated meant that we were able to think in a way that our clients couldn't. It was this thinking that allowed us to make the best recommendations, give the best advice, and get the best outcome. As lawyers, even after we'd spent time thinking about our client's case, we'd always discuss it with colleagues for their perspectives and insights. Multiple brains are better than one (so long as they're the right brains for the job in hand), especially with important and often complex situations. This is why I will always be an advocate for prioritising the way you think in business, both behind the scenes and in public.

Thinking is a valuable skill. Sound decisions are made as a result of thorough thinking. And yet this skill seems to be underrated in the online space where the focus is on producing (content, offers, results, more content) and the answer to any roadblocks along the way is usually to "work on your mindset". Mindset work is great, but it's not the same as deliberate thinking, both strategically and creatively. And that's where I believe a great opportunity lies in online business. While other brands do what they do and exist in the epidemic of generic, you can brand the way you think and put yourself in a category of one. People come to you for results, of course, but more so because of who you are and the way you get those results. That's a consequence of your being and your thinking.

Before we explore the four brand authority profiles, these are the assumptions I've made as a baseline for all:

- You're smart and you consider yourself a lifelong learner (some might argue you're addicted to "self-development" but you don't mind that – there are worse drugs to take!).
- You're a legit expert at something.

- Your work facilitates excellent results for people.
- You're resourceful and have a history of betting on yourself.
- You're curious, thoughtful, and deliberate in your decision-making.

You can self-select your primary profile based on the descriptions in this chapter. You may feel a stronger pull towards one category and still recognise parts of yourself in another. That's normal! We're complex beings who don't fit perfectly in boxes.

THE HIDDEN GEM

The first authority profile is the Hidden Gem. Hidden Gems possess a borderline-dangerous combination of expertise, wisdom, and qualities that make them exceptional at what they do. They set themselves a standard of excellence and always deliver. (And if they don't, they always put it right.) Clients constantly tell them how brilliant they are, and referrals are easy to come by. They're smart (and always getting smarter because they're obsessed with sharpening their minds and skills), wildly capable, and lead themselves with integrity. Hidden Gems work with *some* great clients who respect the way they think and pay without hesitation, but they'd really love more of them – or the same amount at higher rates.

The challenge of the Hidden Gem is that while they're an undeniable expert, not enough people know about it. They've inadvertently got caught in the epidemic of generic. They don't want to contribute to the noise online, but as a result, *they've diluted the power of their presence*. They're shining in a sparse room. They feel like the best-kept secret of their industry while their competitors seem to be lapping up the clients and visibility opportunities they'd be a perfect match for. They try not to compare themselves to said competitors, but it's tough at times. Hidden Gems may have a more reserved presence because they often fall more on the introverted side of the spectrum but when I say Hidden Gem, I don't (necessarily) mean they're hiding. They could be highly visible, but if they're not saying what they truly want to say or selling what they truly want to sell, they'll never feel truly seen.

The Hidden Gem's thinking trap is thinking deeply but not taking enough bold action. Their intellect is one of the reasons Hidden Gems are so exceptional at what they do. But spending too much time thinking and perfecting and not enough time deciding and *doing* is keeping them from building the lifetime legacy they secretly tell themselves they want to create. The industry loves to label Hidden Gems as "overthinkers" and that can be interpreted and internalised as something negative. In reality, Hidden Gems are *deep* thinkers, which is a beautiful and important thing, but it's only worth the mental energy if they act on their thinking – even if it's at a slower pace. Deep thinking can escalate into overthinking when they're contemplating the same issues, over and over, without changing any of the circumstances. If they don't change the circumstances, it's hard to change the thinking, so, their results will stagnate.

Hidden Gems have a tendency to perpetually polish their ideas before letting them see the light of day, and as a result, few ever do. They sometimes mistake their standard of excellence for a standard of perfection, which is, of course, impossible to meet, and they (wrongly) believe they need to fill knowledge gaps before being ready to take action. This thinking trap often means Hidden Gems hoard their best ideas, don't make moves to bring their original thoughts to life through offers, assets, and content (and then fume when they see someone else do the exact thing they've been thinking about), and don't build an outer authority that matches their inner authority.

THE MESSY MOVER

The second authority profile is the Messy Mover. Messy Movers have the huge asset of relentless ambition. They have a smoking-hot blend of expertise, wisdom, and other qualities that mean getting what they want is not optional. Their clients are consistently in awe of the way they get stuff done – and get the results. They're cunningly resourceful, willing to experiment, and always seem to land on their feet (with money in their bank account). Messy Movers are the imperfect action-takers who run like the wind with an idea. They may not know what or where the finish line is exactly, but they don't wait to figure that out first. They either have enough evidence of other people's success, enough faith in their own abilities, or a blend of the two to trust that taking scrappy action is going to serve them better than staying still. For that reason, while they still hold their work to a certain standard, they don't struggle with perfectionism.

The challenges? While Messy Movers find it natural to make big, bold, beautiful moves, they're not always in service to their personality, capacity, and ultimate vision. They've inadvertently got caught in the epidemic of generic. They want to stand out, but as a result of pursuing all their ideas, *they've diluted the power of their best ones.* They feel like they're building something they can't keep up with, and they want more ease in signing dream clients and getting epic visibility opportunities.

The Messy Mover's thinking trap is spending too much time doing and not enough time thinking. Their courageous scrappiness is one of the reasons Messy Movers have already created so much success for themselves, and action is a way of processing what they think (though they may not realise this). But spending too much time doing and not enough time thinking about whether these are the best actions to take or *continue taking* is keeping them from building the lifetime legacy they tell everyone they want to create. Messy Movers have a tendency to tie their internal worth to their external actions and results and struggle to find satisfaction in whatever they achieve. They're onto the next goal before celebrating hitting their previous one. Even though they're highly motivated to produce, the ultimate creation may feel like a by-product of force rather than flow. Messy Movers may have a more noticeable presence because they often fall more on the extroverted side of the spectrum.

This is typically the trap that leads to burnout. Messy Movers can find themselves saying, *"If this is what's required to get that, I'm not sure I want it,"* but keep going anyway. They can end up expending a huge amount of energy doing things that don't actually make either short-term or long-term sense. For example, creating a new low-ticket offer because it's trendy rather than because it serves their bigger picture business strategy and fitting within their existing offer ecosystem and energetic capacity. Their focus is on doing (because that's how many of us have been programmed), and the bulk of the thinking happens in hindsight. They might learn lessons, but did they even need to? Sometimes, as a Messy Mover, there is a better path available, but they've moved so fast they didn't even realise it was there.

THE LOST REBEL

The third authority profile is the Lost Rebel. Lost Rebels have a habit of approaching much of life and business both differently and excellently. They're enigmas full of expertise, wisdom, and other such qualities that mean challenging conventions are in their DNA. Their clients are obsessed with the work they do together and describe them as their secret weapon. Lost Rebels are naturally creative. They constantly innovate on their own ideas and their dedication to change-making is enviable. Maintaining uniqueness and agency is incredibly important to their identity. If they're not doing things differently, those things are probably not worth doing.

The Lost Rebel's challenge is that while *they* know the immense power of their work, it can be tricky to communicate it to those who would actually benefit from it. They've inadvertently got caught in the epidemic of generic. Their greatest gifts can sometimes be misunderstood, and it leads them to question where they truly fit in the landscape of life and business. They have a depth that few are able to recognise which can result in an emotional pendulum. They're certain of so much... and uncertain of so much more. Lost Rebels have massive value to offer, but it feels like it gets lost in translation, sometimes to the point where they forget their magic, seek external validation for their ideas, and make decisions from a wobbly place. They recoil at the idea of squashing themselves into messaging formulas or step-by-step processes but still find themselves wondering if it would actually be the answer to their problems. They know they need to be able to clearly articulate their brilliance if they're going to get noticed by more of the clients they'd pinch themselves to work with and build a stellar reputation – especially now that AI has joined the chat.

The Lost Rebel's trap is thinking in a vacuum. Their unique way of seeing the world is why the Lost Rebel's work creates such impact-generating results. But spending too much time ideating solo and not enough time packaging and communicating their wisdom in ways that make the right people say *"Yes, I need that!"* is keeping them from building the lifetime legacy they strive to create. While the Lost Rebel prioritises thinking time on their business, they only have their own brain for company. This is fine initially, but without a skilled sounding board to throw their thinking at, they'll only have their own lenses to work with. This is naturally limiting and may lead to challenges down the road simply because they hadn't considered something they didn't have awareness of but could have. They say you can't read the label from inside the jar. Lost Rebels don't need someone to understand everything about them, but they do need someone to reflect their brilliance back to them.

THE IRRESISTIBLE AUTHORITY

The fourth and final authority profile is the Irresistible Authority – a surprisingly rare breed. This is who the Hidden Gem, Messy Mover, and Lost Rebel have the potential and aspiration to be. Irresistible Authorities know how to balance strategy and creativity. They are deliberate thinkers and daring doers. When you're the Irresistible Authority:

- You have a Rolodex of clients who buy, share, and love on you consistently.
- You get industry-leading results doing work that lights you up.
- You've developed a reliable reputation that sees your inbox fizzing with quality enquiries, speaking requests, and guest expert invitations.
- You become The One rather than one of many.
- You're seen as the must-have in your market.
- You're sought-after and in-demand by the right people.
- You can charge a premium.
- You're able to be fully self-expressed.
- People binge your body of work.
- People listen to you and respect your perspectives even if they disagree.
- You turn your unique ideas into desirable assets.
- You have a competitive edge that people come to know you for.
- You gain more traction by doing less.
- Your audience becomes hooked on you.
- Dream clients turn up on your doorstep.
- You're referred and recommended more, even by people you don't know.
- Sales conversations convert easily.
- You become known for ideas you own.
- You have a deeply resonant presence.
- Exciting growth and visibility opportunities seem to land in your lap.
- You increase the lifetime value of your clients.
- Your audience grows in both size and adoration.
- You feel peace in your visibility.

- You're unwavering in the way you show up in the world.

Thought leader *plus* desirable offer *equals* irresistible authority.

THE OBVIOUS CHOICE IS NOT THE GOAL

The more sophisticated the market becomes the more discerning people are in their decision-making. I want you to be the best choice for the right people, but that doesn't necessarily mean you'll be the *obvious* choice. At least, not from the beginning. If you want incredible clients, expect them to do their due diligence. It's your job to make it as easy as possible for your ideal clients to understand why it's in their best interests to choose you – and be detached if they choose differently. Maybe you're thinking: *I don't believe in competition.* A great attitude, but a naive one. Yes, you're unique, but that doesn't make you immune to competition. Branding the way you think isn't about eliminating competition so there is none, it's about making the competition irrelevant so that you become the chosen one. And even if what you do *is* so incredibly specialist that you don't have competitors, you are still competing for the right people's attention in a world littered with distractions.

Demand and desire only matter if you're building it in the people you love to work with. You want to be chosen by those who will thrive when working with you. It's *your* job to translate your wisdom and articulate it in a way that speaks to dream clients only. There's a tipping point where branding what you do becomes branding how you think. That's when you stop speaking to those who are only interested in getting a result and start speaking to those who are on your intellectual wavelength; who respect what you do, yes, but also *why* and *how* you guide them to a result. These are dream clients. When you've already got demand and a reputation, *you* have to decide how to package and present your wisdom.

Let's get you crystal clear on exactly what you want to be known for and how to translate that into power perspectives, proprietary framework, positioning concept, and presence strategy that creates a deep and rippling impact, builds a new level of authority, has you commanding higher rates for access to your wisdom, and solidifies you as your dream client's next obsession.

3

ESCAPING THE EPIDEMIC OF GENERIC

Have you ever taken advice from someone you admire only to realise (too late) that what's true for them simply isn't true for you? As a result, you've set yourself back who-knows-how-long by listening to them, like a "good girl", instead of listening to that feeling in your gut whispering: *No, this is wrong for you.*

A few years ago, I dropped a cool five figures on a high-level mastermind run by a legend of the copywriting industry. It was a huge deal. I remember how profusely my armpits were sweating when I pressed the buy button, but the excitement I had for being in this brilliant expert's presence quashed the voice that kept rising in my mind saying: *She's encouraging you to turn you into someone you're not.* The advice?

- Ditch working for creatives (who were my main client base).

- Remove references to creativity from your marketing because copywriting is about data and conversions, not creativity (which was my main strength).
- Your clients loving the copy you write for them is irrelevant (which was my main kind of feedback).

So, I shifted my messaging away from creatives. I switched from marketing myself as a creative copywriter to a conversion copywriter. I stopped looking for emotion-driven feedback for my work and sure, I had some success. I had "Celebrity" clients and referrals, my most lucrative project to date, creating copy for six-figure launches… But all this came at the cost of:

- My favourite kind of clients – now people would come to me because they just wanted their copy to convert, not because they wanted unique language to represent them and their brand.
- The joy I had for my work – all data and no fun makes Suzi a very bored human, and I thought that people would only see me as a true pro if my work was data-driven, not personality-driven.
- The feedback that made me dance around my kitchen with wild abandon – the words: "We'll test it" are way less of a turn-on than: "I love it!"

It's understandable to feel a compulsion to take advice from those you look up to. They're at the top of the game, and you want a taste of what it's like to be there. They've been around longer, so surely, they know better. You've paid for access to their genius, so you'd be a fool not to do as they say and follow in their footsteps. It's why it stings even more when you realise that the advice that was meant to propel you closer to your big vision has only taken you closer to someone else's.

This is a classic example of building a brand around what you do rather than who you are and how you think. It's all too common in the online space, which is why we're surrounded by same-same messaging, shallow promises, regurgitated content, and hype marketing, regardless of niche. I call this the epidemic of generic. In the online space, where every market seems saturated, niching feels like an Olympic sport, and we're bombarded by content clawing for our precious attention every time we have a screen in front of us, it's all too easy to get stuck in the epidemic of generic – a crowded place where everything seems to have been seen and said before. What was original is now commonplace. What was novel is now boring. What was captivating is now old news. The online industry has grown and is continuing to grow at an astronomical pace. Standing out has become a more complex challenge, which is why finding a way to rise to it is more important than ever.

THE SEVEN SYMPTOMS

I've identified seven symptoms you may be experiencing a blend of that are keeping you stuck in the epidemic of generic.

1. Should obedience: Following what An Important Person said you should do, even if it goes against your instincts and better judgment.
2. Guru mimicking: Not-quite-cloning what other (seemingly) more successful people are doing because you hope it will bring you the same kinds of results.

3. Genius hoarding: Keeping your brilliant ideas behind closed doors, polishing, perfecting, reserving them for another time.
4. Message dilution: Censoring yourself and what you really want to say to appease the masses and avoid ruffling any egos.
5. Echo chambering: Regurgitating popular or highly engaged with content, thereby trapping yourself in a bubble of same-same ideas.
6. Hype marketing: Promoting your offers based on hype, look-at-me lifestyle content, and shallow promises.
7. Visual blandscaping: Keeping the way your brand looks absent of any distinctive personality ("Beige is my favourite colour" said nobody, ever... Except me, when I'm at my favourite bakery choosing lunch). Branding goes far beyond logos, colours and graphics, as I'm sure you know, but as I'm not a visual brand expert, I've chosen not to explore this further in this book.

These seven symptoms are signs you're too focused on expertise, outcome, and appearing a certain way, versus wisdom, perspective, and the full expression of who you are. Let's take a look at these in more detail so you can identify where you might be getting tangled in the epidemic of generic – and then we can plot your escape together.

SHOULD OBEDIENCE

From the moment we leave the womb, we learn what to do from others. We model behaviour. We're literally a product of our parenting. Then we go to school where we're programmed to obey and to follow the rules, even when we don't understand why the rules exist. Our quirks are often seen as inconveniences, and our edges are dismissed or neglected until they're blunt; the exact same quirks and edges that become our superpowers in business, if we let them. When we've been programmed to obey in one area of life, it's easy to transfer that programming to another. So, when we build a business, we look to someone in a position of authority to tell us what to do. There's nothing wrong with this. I wouldn't be where I am today were it not for the guidance of coaches, mentors, and consultants. What *is* wrong is when their wisdom contradicts your own and obeying their "should" requires ignoring your intuition – the very thing that will never steer you wrong.

Should obedience is following what An Important Person said you *should* do, even if it goes against your instincts and better judgment. I've lost count of the number of conversations I've had with people who have obeyed other people's "shoulds" against their own internal compass because they felt they had to, and then paid the mental, emotional, energetic, or financial price later down the line. You should have a client avatar. You should have a funnel. You should have *this* kind of funnel. You should launch. You should do evergreen. You should ditch sales calls. You should fill your calendar with sales calls. You should twerk on TikTok. You should take payment over the phone before they've signed a contract. You should only have one offer. You should have multiple offers, so no money is left on the table. The should isn't right or wrong. What matters is whether it's right or wrong *for you*. The truth is it can all work. People teach (and therefore earn money for) what works for them. It doesn't mean it will work for you. It doesn't mean it *should* work for you. It's your job to discern the difference between what's aligned and in integrity for your advisors and what's aligned and in integrity for you.

I remember being thrown out of A Level English class because I told the teacher I wouldn't be submitting another assignment until I'd had feedback on my previous one. It made no sense to me to put time and effort into a paper if I didn't know where I needed to improve. Naturally, he erupted like a bald volcano. He got so close to my face I could smell his anger. The head of year called my house (unusual), and I was asked to apologise so it could all blow over. I refused. Why should I apologise? Just because he was in a position of authority did not make him right. Everything in my body and mind told me that I needed to trust what I felt was right. If obeying him meant disobeying my sense of self, it wasn't worth it. (I never returned to his class, and I got an A on my final exam, which was a great middle finger moment for me.)

It's worth noting that not wanting to try something simply because it feels scary doesn't necessarily mean it's not the right move. Wisdom also means knowing the difference between misalignment and resistance. If you're not sure, experiment. Let yourself play. Then plug into the way your mind and body respond. Self-leadership doesn't happen without listening.

GURU MIMICKING

The irony of building a personal brand based on someone else. It's laughable, and yet it happens all the time. People see someone they admire, put them and their perceived success on a pedestal, and then think that copycatting is either a requirement or a shortcut to the same success. It comes back to the point that who you are is not enough, and so, you try somebody else on for size to see how they fit. Hint: they never fit. They say imitation is the sincerest form of flattery... *Until you get sued for it.* While I say that with my tongue firmly in my cheek, it's a real possibility when you work on the internet. As a personal brand, you're selling a version of yourself. You are the asset, the face, and the product. You're packaging your skills, knowledge, ideas, and experience in a way that solves problems and being paid for it. If someone comes along and imitates it – imitates *you* – they're not only taking something that doesn't belong to them, but they're also asking for something that is rightfully yours.

Guru mimicking is not quite cloning what other (seemingly) more successful people are doing because you hope it will bring you the same kinds of results. It could be dressing up one of their ideas in a slightly different outfit, or it could be literally dressing like them. This happens because the "guru" has what they want. They already have the success, the riches, the lifestyle. When you're smart, and you enjoy educating yourself, your brain looks for evidence. And they are evidence of what's possible. The question is whether you use that evidence to innovate or imitate. When you don't have enough faith in yourself to innovate, you often imitate. The brain starts to think: *If they've reached this level by doing X, then I should probably do X too.* What people don't realise in some cases (at least not right away), is that they aren't just imitating a process, they're imitating an identity. It's like should obedience but you're putting the should on yourself.

Beyond any legal ramifications, the danger of guru mimicking lies in rooting for the guru more than you root for yourself. Putting them on any kind of pedestal immediately adjusts your self-concept so you see yourself as beneath them.

And their apparent success or appearance of perfection makes it so that you want to become more like them versus becoming more of yourself. Inspiration is cool. Imitation is not. A creation you pass off as your own will never contain the same energetic charge as one that truly is your own. One of my former mentors once said to me, you never want to meet your heroes because you'll realise, they're just normal people. Recognise the traits they have that you admire. They're a mirror of what's *already* within you, but your success will be a result of extracting and expressing your own wisdom, not theirs.

GENIUS HOARDING

I consider myself a recovering perfectionist. If I didn't have a publishing deadline for this book, it would probably still be in my laptop drafts. Perfectionism is rife in online business, often plaguing the most talented minds. It's not enough to have talent; you have to *trust* it. And perfection loves to trick us into believing we have to meet an impossible standard before our work is good enough to be seen.

Genius hoarding is keeping your brilliant ideas behind closed doors, polishing, perfecting, and reserving them for another time. There are a few reasons this happens. The most common is that you fear the negative feedback that's a risk with any kind of creation, despite your conscious mind knowing that even globally recognised masterpieces have haters. Does that mean the world is better off without them? No. You are separate from your ideas. Rejection of an idea you created is not the same as rejection of you as a human. You may also worry that if you share your best ideas, you'll run out of them. Great ideas breed. When one is shared, space is created for another to grow. Perhaps you have concerns about your ideas being copied. This simply demonstrates how valuable you believe your ideas to be. Is it a risk? Sure. But what if it's riskier to hoard them? If that value never sees the light of day, if it eats you up from the inside, you'll never feel fully self-expressed, and your people will never get to experience being changed by it. Self-expression requires surrender. It can be uncomfortable, but not more uncomfortable than keeping your genius locked in a mental goldmine.

MESSAGE DILUTION

"Coke please, no ice." I receive a drink filled with ice and proceed to either send it back or fish all the cubes out with a fork and hide them somewhere. This is me at every restaurant. I hate ice. And not just because I'm allergic to the cold, but because it dilutes my darn drink. Dilution is the action of making something weaker. Message dilution is censoring yourself and what you really want to say to appease the masses and avoid ruffling any egos. Examples include:

- Sanitising what you really want to say for fear of disagreement, judgment, or being misunderstood.
- Communicating to multiple audiences at the same time because you think casting the net wider to meet people at different stages of the buying journey will result in a better catch.
- Squeezing your unique perspectives into templates or formulas that strip the power from them.

Dilution isn't what creates obsession; potency is. If you're concerned your message is boring, it probably is. Not because *you're* boring, but because you're keeping up appearances.

Diluting your message is out of integrity. You're not in congruence with your truth, and you're not reaching the people you could help. Find the depth. Find the difference. Share from a place of power. Your message is not meant for the masses. Stop communicating like it is.

ECHO CHAMBERING

You've heard the phrase, *"I can't hear myself think,"* maybe in relation to being somewhere noisy, where the buzz is so loud that your internal narrative gets drowned out. But have you considered this is exactly what's happening when you're mindlessly consuming information online? Echo chambering is regurgitating popular or highly engaged with content, thereby trapping yourself in a bubble of same-same ideas. I know you love learning, and it's smart to keep an eye on what others in your industry are doing. But at what cost? When you prioritise devouring other people's perspectives, you leave less space for developing your own *unless* you're consuming in a conscious way.

Trust your mind to create new perspectives rather than regurgitating or repackaging what already exists. It's easy to do when the same ideas, messages, and promises seem to be rattling around you all day long. They start to become so common it's easy to think you have to join the echo chamber to even be heard. You don't. But you do have to turn the volume down on their voices to better hear your own… And then trust it enough to say something the world isn't used to hearing.

HYPE MARKETING

Let it be known that saying, *"I am so excited! You cannot miss out on this!!!"* is not an effective marketing strategy. Well, it might be for people who have already got a huge audience and a strong reputation. And that's the real issue. Once you've *built* the audience and the reputation, you can make pretty much any offer and it will sell. The trust has been established. The social proof is there. If you don't yet have the brand authority that makes you undeniably relevant, trying to lead a promotion with excitement versus genuine substance isn't going to work. You're not selling your feelings; you're solving problems.

Hype marketing activates a FOMO response, and this isn't how you want to begin a client relationship. We want people to make decisions from a grounded, certain, steady place, not because they feel like they're going to regret their decision if they don't pull the trigger right now – or they may end up regretting pulling the trigger instead. The same can be said if you're trying to use your lifestyle to market something. First-class holidays and bougie handbags might be aspirational but they aren't reasons for someone to buy from you, that's just showing people what you're about to spend their money on. If you see others doing this, ask yourself whether it's because they're flaunting what their expertise has made possible for them (totally cool) or whether it's because they're hiding behind the fact that their expertise is average.

Some of the worst marketing advice I've heard is: *Build it and they will come*. No, in the vast majority of cases, they won't. You need to translate your wisdom in a way that helps someone understand the distinct value of it. If you can't do this, your brand might build popularity, but it won't build authority. The most reliable kind of campaigns are built on truth, not hype.

THE ESCAPE

The fish ate my vomit. I know that's not a conventional way to end a chapter but we're not conventional beings, so let's roll with it. It was 2013 and I was on holiday with my then-boyfriend in Koh Lanta, Thailand. By some stroke of malign luck, the weather was abysmal. Seeing as I couldn't lie on a beach getting a tan that would disappear as soon as I was home, I enrolled myself on a scuba diving course. After doing our sessions in the pool, we were whisked off on a speedboat to a gorgeous dive site. The problem? The storms made the sea ultra-choppy, and it turns out I get disgustingly seasick. Being sick off the side of a boat is not a vibe. I can confirm this because my then-boyfriend took photos to show me afterwards. For some reason, I later married him. Despite the huge waves, I decided it was easier for me to be in the water itself, clinging to a buoy like a barnacle while I retched into the sea and watched as the fish gathered around me to snaffle what I'd had for breakfast.

Being stuck on the surface, where the waves were tumultuous, the ride was rough, and everything was noisy, blurred, and *not-at-all-fun*, resulted in me feeling way too sorry for myself considering how much I'd pay to do this course. But when I dived underneath the surface? Everything changed. The deeper I went, the calmer the sea, the clearer my mind, and the steadier my stomach. If you haven't dived before, I can only describe it as being part of an alternative universe, a vividly peaceful world where there is no noise to compete with. There's safety in the shallows, but a dangerous amount of opportunity in the depths.

It's fascinating that we spend our whole lives trying to fit in until we start a business and then we spend our whole lives trying to stand out. So, why does this epidemic of generic exist? Because while a lot of business owners *say* they want to stand out, they then spend an inordinate amount of time doing the opposite. It's understandable when you think that, in life, we're ultimately seeking belonging. There's safety in numbers. There's comfort in a crowd. There's proof in what's generic.

Originality requires defiance. Which is why we don't see all that much of it. It's one thing to say that you don't want to do things the way everyone else is, but it's quite another to actually do things differently. I know too many brilliant business owners hiding the best of their brains because they've reached a crossroads. Do they choose what already exists? Or do they finally choose themselves? Uniqueness in their business is so important to them that following the crowd would feel like doing their soul a disservice. Not a long-term option. But to pioneer a new path? Well, that feels tempting but terrifying. What if nobody's interested in that path? What if that path is lonely? What if that path takes so much longer to walk? These are all real possibilities but if I know you, you're at the point where you're ready to make the choice. You either defy yourself, or you defy the paths already paved. The truth is both are uncertain. Both contain unknowns. But only one will take you on the journey you're looking for.

4

WISDOMBRANDING

"*I've got most of the puzzle pieces, I'm just not sure exactly how to put them together in the right way.*" I hear a version of this every week from my clients (or people who should be my clients).

The puzzle pieces include a variety of:

- Undeniable expertise.
- Interesting industry perspectives.
- Fresh ideas.
- Unique frameworks.
- Stories.
- Positioning concepts.
- Compelling messaging.
- Irresistible offers.
- Authority assets.
- Strong presence.

The right way is the way that:

- Establishes you as an authority in a category of one.
- Captivates more of your favourite clients and visibility opportunities.
- Feels more like you than ever before.

It's all too easy to think that once you have the puzzle pieces put together in a nice, neat way, everything is going to be perfect. I hate to break it to you, but it won't be. Not (necessarily) because you've got the wrong pieces, but because the puzzle will never be complete. You, your brand, your business, isn't some hundred-piece, out-of-the-box job. The puzzle will forever evolve and expand as you do. It's why you feel like you've outgrown what you've created almost as soon as you've created it. It's why you believe there must be "something else" before you feel complete. It's why you aren't showing up as the irresistible authority already, fully self-expressed, leading with conviction, and taking *ownership* of the brilliance in your brain, even though you know deep in your bones you're meant to be. Yes, you're a masterpiece in the making, but the masterpiece will never actually be or feel complete. The sooner you embrace that, the easier it will become to evolve your personal brand in a way that makes a real, rippling impact.

WisdomBranding is turning the gold in your mind into the gold in your bank account. It's a way to monetise your ideas by stoking desire and driving demand for your offers. It's about branding the way you think and articulating it with conviction, so you're positioned in a league of your own, and it's about tuning into and trusting your own wisdom when making decisions in your business. Wisdom is a collection of expertise, ideas, stories, skills, and lessons. Branding is the way you package and present that to the world. This is the creative part. Creativity is a muscle. It needs time under tension to grow, to flourish, to compound, but as humans in a world full of urgency, convenience, and instant gratification, we don't want to spend the time, and we don't want to experience the tension. But the more you:

- Avoid the discomfort of boredom;
- Turn to AI to do the thinking for you;
- Rely on following the "proven pathways" of your peers and mentors;
- Suppress what's true and replace it with what's trendy;
- Look to templates and formulas to help you articulate your wisdom and communicate your value...

... the less you're tensing your creative muscle. Which means that over time, it will become weaker and weaker until you feel completely disconnected from it. This is how you fall out of love with your business. Creativity isn't a requirement to make sales, but it is a requirement if you want to be recognised as an irresistible authority in your industry, respected as a distinct voice, loved as a leader, and paid for your perspective.

CAN'T GET YOU OUT OF MY HEAD

You want to be recognised and rewarded by the right people for your big ideas? Position yourself accordingly. Just like you have a brand, whether you've created it intentionally or not, you're also positioned a certain way whether you've done it intentionally or not. Positioning is the strategic art of creating a mental association with your brand. It's how you're perceived in the mind of your market in relation to your competitors. This is why the topic of positioning always comes down to what makes you different from those competitors. The instinctive mental association that your difference creates is a huge contributing factor as to why someone will or will not buy from you. When you find the right way to be distinctive, you'll build brand authority and affinity with ease.

Positioning is still subjective. We can make decisions to help shape the perception we desire others to have, but we can't guarantee it. It's why one person can look at a brand and think it's an expensive luxury and another person can look at the same brand and think it's affordable. It's why one person can rave about the exceptional experience they have with a brand and another person can complain about it. The important piece is knowing who your right person is and positioning your brand with *them* in mind. If that person evolves, your positioning should evolve too.

Framing is a way of influencing perception by highlighting or downplaying certain aspects of a brand. The way information is presented plays a huge part in how people respond to it. Our brains are wired to save calories, and framing helps us shortcut our thinking. In his book *Hemlock Grove*, Brian McGreevy states: *"If a problem can't be solved within the frame it was conceived, the solution lies in reframing the problem."* You've heard the phrase *frame of reference*. That's exactly what helps you shape perception. It's like saying: *"I'm the Rolls Royce of marketing consultants."* The Rolls Royce is the frame, which brings up associations of expensive, exclusive, luxury, prestige, etc. What matters is that the associations you highlight influence the way your ideal clients think about your brand.

The same thing that will attract one person will repel another. That's exactly what we want. The whole point of branding the way you think is to help influence the way your market thinks (and feels). Your job is to create the kinds of mental associations that connect with the values, beliefs, and desires of the people you most want to work with. You don't make your competition irrelevant by shouting louder; you do it by saying the things they're not and presenting your brand in interesting ways.

There are many ways brands can choose to position themselves.

- Values
- Results
- Price (do not recommend this one!)
- Approach
- Speed
- Convenience
- Experience
- Innovation

As a personal brand, your wisdom is its own category. You don't need to be the first, the best, or the only one in any other category when you lead with the gold in your mind.

THE WISDOMBRANDING FRAMEWORK

In the next section of this book, I'm going to take you through my proprietary WisdomBranding framework which will show you how to use the brilliance in your brain to position you as the irresistible authority and the must-have in your market.

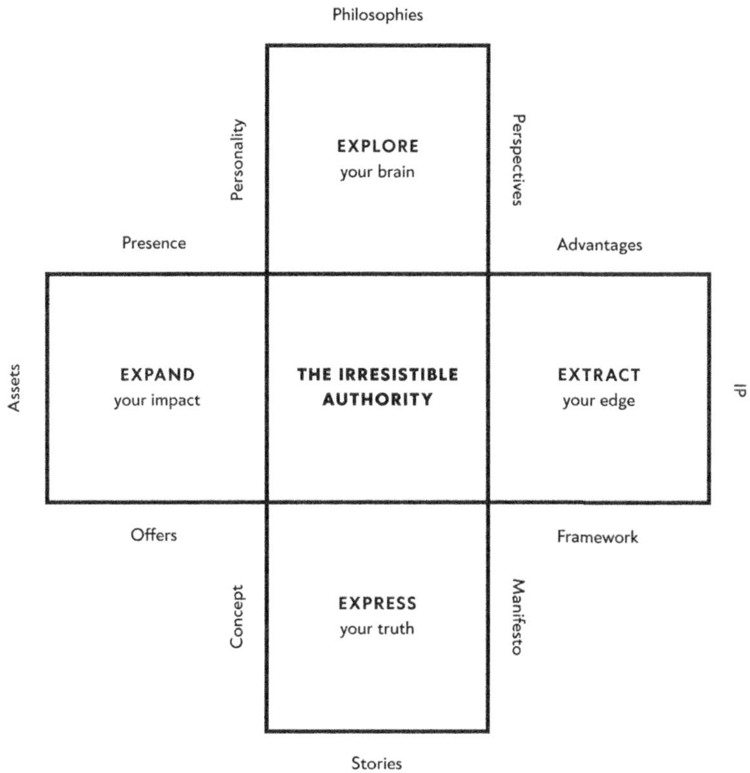

1 EXPLORE YOUR BRAIN

Personality: Curate an intriguing identity that's based on you without requiring all of you.

Philosophies: Delve into the personal values, beliefs, and ideals that make you who you are and see how they shape the leader you're becoming.

Perspectives: Uncover the unique way you see the work you do in the world, and why those viewpoints are the doorway to connecting powerfully with your ideal audience.

Core outcome: power perspectives.

2 EXTRACT YOUR EDGE

Advantages: Translate your unique essence, expertise, and experience into reasons why people desire to work with you above anybody else.

IP: Turn your most valuable ideas into irresistible and uncopyable concepts that allow people to understand how your brilliance can help them.

Framework: Structure your intuitive approach to what you do in a simple yet potent proprietary model that helps you instantly elevate your positioning.

Core outcome: proprietary framework.

3 EXPRESS YOUR TRUTH

Manifesto: Clarify your thought leader mission and turn it into a manifesto that amplifies your distinct voice and activates your dream clients.

Stories: Articulate your wisdom with transparency, integrity, and conviction through content that deeply resonates with your audience.

Concept: Find a compelling angle that pulls your wisdom together in a way you can creatively infuse into your brand communications.

Core outcome: positioning concept.

4 EXPAND YOUR IMPACT

Offers: Develop a deliciously positione
allows you to provide a high level of impact in
respects your energetic capacity and lifestyle desires.

Assets: Infuse your genius into authority assets (website, podcasts, books, keynotes, etc.) that get you recognised and rewarded on a more significant scale.

Presence: Exude authority in a way that feels good with a powerful and peaceful presence that captivates the right clients and opportunities.

Core outcome: presence strategy.

Your power perspectives become your messaging.
Your proprietary framework becomes your brand backbone.
Your positioning concept becomes your creative direction.
Your presence strategy becomes the way you call in the right people.

If you want to become the irresistible authority, I recommend you upgrade all four.

PHASE 1: EXPLORE YOUR BRAIN

They've just started talking about an idea almost identical to the one you had a few months ago but kept to yourself. Admit it, you're envious – not in a wishing-them-ill kind of way (that's not you at all!), but in a curious, yet frustrated, *"Why aren't I where they are?"* kind of way. Their presence seems so effortless while showing up and sharing your thought leader perspectives is still something you waver about. (See also: you're not entirely sure what your thought leader perspectives are yet.) They've got a rapturous audience eating out the palm of their well-manicured hands while you believe yours is too small and you've already burned them out talking about your offers. You know they're smart, but they're definitely not smarter than you. What do they have that you don't? Why is this happening? It's not your message, or your offer, or whatever else Important People On The Internet say it is. It's because you're treating your brain like a maze, not a labyrinth.

A maze is designed to confuse. There are dead ends, false starts, and multiple ways to reach the middle. A labyrinth, while just as intricate as a maze, has only one path leading to the centre, and the same path leads back out. Maybe you've heard of the Greek myth of Theseus and the Minotaur. Theseus is a prince who is ordered into an underground labyrinth as a sacrificial tribute to King Minos. A Minotaur lies in wait at the centre. Before he leaves, King Minos's daughter falls in love with Theseus and gives him a ball of golden thread to help him find his way out of the labyrinth. Theseus fixes one end of the thread to the entrance of the labyrinth and unrolls it as he ventures inside. He reaches the centre, kills the Minotaur, and uses the golden thread to retrace his steps and escape.

Right now, there is so much *in* your brain that you get lost in it. How can you possibly translate all of your brilliance into one simple yet sophisticated brand? Your brain is not designed to be a maze of confusion. It's a labyrinth of wisdom with one clear through-line. Your job is to explore the labyrinth, find and follow the through-line, and use it to propel your online presence in a bolder direction. That's what the people you're envious of have done. Found and followed their golden thread for long enough to position themselves as an authority.

PHASE 1 OF THE WISDOMBRANDING FRAMEWORK: EXPLORE YOUR BRAIN

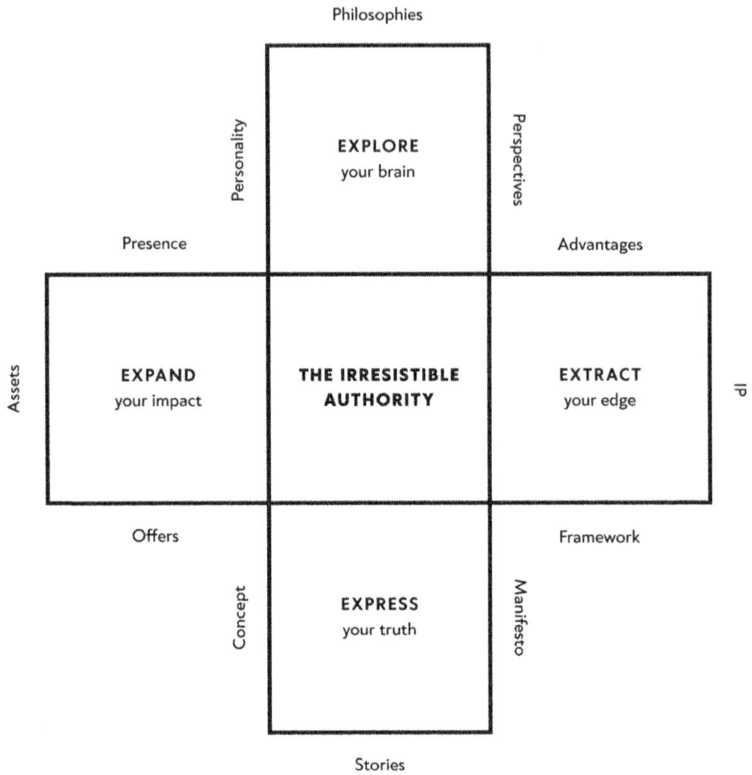

Personality: Curate an intriguing identity that's based on you without requiring all of you.

Philosophies: Delve into the personal values, beliefs, and ideals that make you who you are and see how they shape the leader you're becoming.

Perspectives: Uncover the unique way you see the work you do in the world, and why those viewpoints are the doorway to connecting powerfully with your ideal audience.

Core phase outcome: power perspectives.

Exploring your brain is how you escape the perplexity of what your personal brand is supposed to be in this noisy online world and use it as your foundation to escape the epidemic of generic. It's not about the visuals – that's a small but important part of building your brand. It's about how you feel when you express yourself through it. When you feel clear and confident, your dream clients will too. Your brand isn't based on design trends, it's based on deep truths.

5

PERSONALITY

In order to shape the desired perception of your brand, you'll want to shape an intriguing identity for yourself that draws the right people in and repels the rest. My acting teacher loves to say: *"Throw away the lines. The words don't matter."* While some teachers focus intensely on the words themselves, he thinks the words don't matter. It's what lies in between the words that is most important. It's what your eyes are doing rather than what your mouth is saying. Intrigue is created in the pauses. This is what forms the context and draws in the audience, not the words themselves. He doesn't believe in characters either. You don't put yourself in the shoes of someone else and become them. You stand in your own shoes and apply different parts of yourself to the material. This is why casting is such a big deal. It's not just about whether someone looks good on screen, or has chemistry with another actor, it's about the way they embody the part by coaxing different pieces of themselves out and allowing them to be seen in a particular way. This is how they take the same script as everyone else but make it their own.

With your personal brand, you're not creating a whole ne character, but you're not "just being yourself" either. You're intentionally shaping your intriguing identity so that when you show up, you connect on a deep level with the right people. You're a credible character based on you. And you get to decide which pieces of yourself you allow to be seen, and how. You're excavating the hidden gold inside you and then being discerning in choosing the pieces you express through your brand. Before you can make those choices, you have to explore what that hidden gold is and recognise what's special about it. To a large extent, your brand is going to reflect your own personality. You are the face of it, and to be authentic, whatever you do and however you show up has to feel like you. I want to reiterate that being authentic does not mean showing all of yourself.

A lot of people I've worked with have said they don't love social media because it feels like a performance. You might be wondering if I'm suggesting your personal brand is a performance. And I'd argue that, to an extent, it is. You're not showing up purely for the fun of it, you're showing up because it's your job. Because if you didn't, your business wouldn't make money. Because if you didn't, you wouldn't reach the people you want to help. Because if you didn't, you wouldn't be a thought leader or an authority. Rather than trying to just be yourself and hoping for the best, *intentionally become a person of interest.*

No matter who you are, you still have a personality that is captivating to certain people. Not *all* people, because that's impossible. We always want to focus on who we're trying to reach with our message, but it's important to note that intentionally becoming a person of interest doesn't mean shaping your personality to fit what you think people want it to be. It the sweet spot between how you want to see ...ow you want others to see you. What does ...elf look like? Your most captivating self? Your ...mfortable self? Your bravest self? Your wisest self? Where are the overlaps? How can you blend traits and characteristics together so that your personal brand has an identity of its own? What are the strongest sides of yourself that you want people to see, connect with, and remember long after they're not in your presence?

People need to be able to root for you so they can root for themselves. They need to see a piece of themselves in you. There's an invisible connection built on values, worldview, and being the embodiment of a leader. If you've ever heard someone say your brand is never about you, it's always about your client, they missed the point. It's always about you *in relation to* what you can do, give, or create for your client.

PUMPKIN YOUR PERSONALITY

One of my favourite books is called *The Pumpkin Plan* by Mike Michalowicz. He explains how certain people dedicate their lives to growing pumpkins. In order to grow the biggest and best pumpkins, they have to sacrifice the rest. It's harsh but effective. It's the same with your brand personality. Being a personal brand doesn't mean you have to be all of yourself online. You can choose the version of yourself that you want to be and put all your efforts into making it shine. What matters is whether the you on the outside is congruent with the you behind closed doors. It's never about exposing everything. It's about making sure the pieces you do choose to show are genuine and will help people feel a connection to you.

Let's look at it another way. Imagine all the elements of your personality are ingredients. There are so many delicious things to choose from. In order to create a delicious dish, would you add *all* of them? Of course not. That would be an overwhelming mess with no distinct flavours. Instead, you would consider what art you want to create, the tastes of those who are hungry, and edit your ingredients accordingly to ensure an excellent experience. You would include elements of familiarity and elements of surprise. There are so many ways you could choose to present your ingredients depending on how you wanted to express yourself and how you wanted the person experiencing your food to feel.

So, how do you decide what your brand personality is? There are a few ways we can approach this. This is where it gets either fun or terrifying depending on, well, your personality. I used to say that I worked with personality-driven brands, now, I prefer to say I work with perspective-driven brands who infuse personality in different ways. You can do that through stories, visuals, conversations, and your overall presence. These kinds of brands put their ideas at the centre rather than their identity. But their identity is important *context*.

INTERROGATE YOURSELF

This is where I recommend you start. It's very much an exploration exercise and you'll need to dig deep to get to the good stuff.

- How would you describe yourself in a sentence?
- What makes you weird?
- What are your quirky habits?

- What are your greatest strengths?
- What gets you ridiculously excited?
- What are your "guilty" pleasures?
- What do you love more than anything?
- Where would I find you when you're not working?
- Where would I never find you?
- When do you feel you are most powerful?
- How do you tend to react to something going wrong?
- What is your favourite thing about yourself?
- Who would play you in a movie?
- What would that movie be called?
- What game do you always win?
- What makes you cry with joy?
- What makes you cry with sadness?
- Has anyone ever said something about your personality that surprised you?
- Is there anything about your personality you wish was different? Why? Could you flip this and turn it into a strength?
- Is there anything about yourself you deliberately hide or keep secret from other people? Why?
- What is it about your personality that you think draws people to you?

Looking back at all your answers, what patterns do you see? What seems intriguing? What can you see in yourself that you don't see in others in your industry? This is a starting place for creating your intriguing identity.

PERSONALITY TEST

Your instinct might be to take a personality test to tell you who you are. Or maybe a quiz to tell you your brand arche-

type. While you could do this (is there anyone who
like a personality test?) it's only going to give you a
put yourself in. The one test I've recommended clients
How To Fascinate®, by Sally Hogshead, because the focus isn't on psychology and how you see yourself; it's based on branding and how the world sees you. The point is to give you tools to impress and influence others. You can use your results to dial up your advantages.

CALL A FRIEND

We're not always in the best position to see all the brilliance inside us, especially when our brilliance is intuitive. Sometimes, the people who know us best can be a mirror and reflect our brilliance back to us. Choose a few friends and clients and ask them to describe you. For friends, simply ask: *What are five personality characteristics or traits you would use to describe me?* For clients, also ask: *What would you consider to be unique/special about me? What did you enjoy most about working with me?*

When you've got your answers, look for surprises. Sometimes the way others see us is not how we see ourselves, and this is all part of building our awareness and curating a brand personality. If we want to shape perception, we want to know what perception has already been shaped.

CREATE YOUR PERSONA

Once you've done the exploration, then you want to create the brand persona. This persona will pull out particular attributes that, when considered together, give people a strong snapshot of what to expect from being in your presence. If an ideal client was going to describe your personality, what would you want them to say? How would you *choose* to be seen? One of my clients once described me as *"cool, calm, and deadly"* and I loved the contrast in those few words, so I added them to my bio. When you know which parts of your personality feel strongest and that you would want to influence the perception of your brand, create a short brand persona. For example: *Suzi likes her bubble baths hot and her humour dry. She's been described as "cool, calm, and deadly" and words are her choice of weapon. Trust her with your brand but not your dessert.*

This persona is something that will come in helpful later on when working on your positioning concept. When you're clear on the personality you want to sprinkle through your brand, you're able to make intentional decisions and take aligned action with that in mind, rather than being influenced by anyone who comes along with an opinion about who you should be.

SHOW ME WHO YOU ARE

It's all Alexandra Franzen's fault. I was on a solo retreat by the coast a few years ago as a Person Who Does Not Drink Coffee, and I read an article of hers which described her dream morning. It included having a coffee machine by her bed so she could make herself a cup without even having to get up. This sounded so delightful that I wanted to try it. There happened to be a Nespresso machine in the cottage I was in, and over the next few days, I became a Person Who Drinks Coffee. I would prepare a morning cup, curl back up in bed with it, and savour it alongside a French macaron as I watched the waves out the window. Literal bliss. By the time

I got home, I had my own machine on order. I'm nothing if not impulsive. Since then, I've had a coffee in bed every morning with my husband, though I've evolved from macarons to Booja Booja chocolate truffles. Now that my son, Alfie, is around, he sits between us and drinks a cup of oat milk. We snuggle, giggle, read books, and talk about life. It's my favourite part of the day. What does this story suggest to you about my personality? Perhaps that I prioritise starting my day with joy. Perhaps that I find joy in beautiful yet ordinary things. Perhaps that my world revolves around my family. Perhaps that I'm lazy? The point is that liking coffee is not a personality trait. Most of the world likes coffee but telling you that doesn't show you anything about who I am or the way I think.

Don't tell me about yourself, *show* me. While other people sell services, you can sell a story. You've probably heard the Maya Angelou quote: *"People won't remember what you did, they'll remember how you made them feel."* It's the blend of your personality, philosophies, and perspectives that will form the foundation of how you make people feel and shape the perception people have of you.

ACTIONS

- Create your three-sentence brand persona.

6

PHILOSOPHIES

I used to be obsessed with a game called The Room. (I don't allow myself to play online escape-the-room games anymore because they suck me in like a Dyson. Ironic.) The game was visually stunning, and one of the key inventory items was a pair of lenses. When you put these on, you could suddenly see something otherwise invisible to you. This is how we go through life. We each have our own collection of life lenses that we wear, never just one at a time. It's the unique *layers* of lenses that allow us to form our worldview. That worldview becomes our wisdom. And it's by sharing that wisdom that we cultivate our thought leadership and connect with the people who are the best fit for our offers.

You don't need to know what all your lenses are. Some will be obvious, such as, I am a white woman, mother, writer, former lawyer, online business owner, introvert etc., others less so. It's more about having the self-awareness that the way you see the world is different from everybody else. Shaping your power perspectives (which we'll be doing in

the next chapter) is a way of helping them see wh
and believe what you believe. Philosophies and pe
are formed as a reaction to something else, filterec
our biases. These are our lenses. Often, we use thes unconsciously. The more self-awareness we cultivate, the easier it becomes to select and switch between lenses to form a perspective in a critical and independent way. We're not trying to eliminate our biases (that would be impossible) but we are giving respect to the fact we have them. We need consumption for inspiration, and the important part is the quality of the consumption. It's smart to consume if we're doing it *intentionally*. The louder the volume of other voices in our head, the more difficult it becomes to hear our own.

The literal definition of philosophy is *"love of wisdom"*. Your personal philosophies are a set of guiding principles, foundational beliefs, values, and attitudes that shape the way you think and act. Your philosophies are a compass for decision-making. If a behaviour is what you do, a philosophy is why you do it. When it comes to branding, the way you see the world is going to be a key factor in helping people understand why they should (or shouldn't) choose to work with you. It's not just because of the way you think as an expert; it's because of the way you think as a *human*. You don't have to be the same as your clients, but you want there to be common threads in your worldviews (and a knowing that even if there were a divergence in belief, it would be handled with emotional intelligence). There must be mutual respect for each other's humanity and expertise. There must be understanding and compassion for the struggles. The people you're going to have the best experience with will be a match for you both philosophically and intellectually. The way we communicate what's important to us will play a huge part in how we're positioned in the minds of our audience.

YOUR REASON FOR BEING

Ikigai is a Japanese word that roughly translates to *"reason for being"*. Our true purpose. The reason we get out of bed every day. This concept inspired Marc Winn to create a Venn diagram which is more suited to business owners. If you do an online search for "ikigai graphic" you'll see there are overlaps between what you love, what the world needs, what you can be paid for, and what you're good at. Everything is connected. If you want to better understand your place in the world, start here. If you want to work with people who are going to be on your wavelength and really invested in working with *you* in particular, these are the things that you want to communicate so people get a strong sense of who you are and what to expect from your presence. Remember, you're building your intriguing identity. You're shaping perception. You want to intentionally draw the right people closer with every move you make.

I BELIEVE IN A WORLD WHERE...

As with the personality chapter, the best way to explore what your philosophies are is to interrogate yourself.

- What do you consider to be important in life?
- What are the personal values you will not compromise on?
- What beliefs do you hold about the world?
- What do you have strong opinions on?
- What are you most passionate or curious about?

- What issues do you simply not care about (even if you're told you should)?
- What makes you angry?
- What would make you lose respect for someone?
- What would make the world a better place?
- What drove you to start your business? Does that same drive remain?
- How do you define or measure success?
- What would you spend money on in a heartbeat?
- What would you never spend money on?
- What situations or conversations make you feel uncomfortable?
- What do you often find yourself disagreeing with people about?
- What could you talk about all day long?

When you've got your answers, what themes do you see? What feels strongest to you? What gives you a fire in your belly? What philosophies do you think you share with your best-fit clients? Create a list of around five core philosophies that sum up what's most important to you. To help you synthesise, you can start by using the sentence, *I believe in a world where…* For example: I believe in a world where quietly rebellious women rise. I believe in a world where women are able to express themselves fully and truthfully, without fear of opportunities being taken away from them, and where it's normal for them to lead the life they've chosen rather than one that's been chosen for them. I believe in a world where courageous expression is modelled for young girls, so they grow up with confidence and resilience running through their veins.

Once you have your core philosophies, turn them into brand behaviours. Identifying beliefs and values makes you a good student. Embodying them makes you a good leader. There is only so much clarity we can find in the confines of our minds. Don't tell me what your values are. Show me. What kind of a leader do you want to be? Do your behaviours reflect that? To continue my example, I do my best to make those philosophies actionable by speaking up and sharing my truth wherever possible, in person or in writing, to show others it's safe to do the same and to be open about both the highs and the lows of walking a more unconventional path. In the future, I want to partner with and donate a portion of my company's profits to organisations that do this kind of work in schools.

ACTIONS

- Curate three-to-five core brand philosophies.
- Translate those into brand behaviours.

7

PERSPECTIVES

Was it blue and black or white and gold? If you remember the dress that went viral, you'll know what I'm talking about. A person posted a photo of a dress online and asked people what colour it was. The world went crackers. Some said it was blue and black. Others insisted it was white and gold. Some saw blue and black one day, then white and gold another day. What was this trickery? How could people *look* at the same thing but *see* it differently? It wasn't about *the* truth; it was *their* truth. This is exactly where our power lies in personal branding. We can look at the same topic, industry, or problem, but see it completely differently. That's how we form our perspectives, and it's those perspectives that give us leverage in the market. If you want to become a thought leader who builds authority and affinity with an audience of buyers and brand ambassadors, you have to actually lead with your thoughts. *Your* thoughts.

If you want to permanently escape the epidemic of generic, take the time to design industry-shifting perspectives. You don't need to follow trends when you can set them. I'm no fashionista, but I'm partial to a bit of Project Runway. The same comment comes up every season: *"Your work must have a point of view."* Fulfil the brief, but make sure we can see who you are as a designer in the garment. If you don't, the judges will say *"I've seen this before..."* and that's the equivalent of being in the epidemic of generic. For contestants, their clothes are the way they express themselves as a designer and connect with their ideal buyers. It's the same with your brand. Captivating brands have a strong point of view. The difference is, yours is communicated through words rather than clothes. If it doesn't have a strong point of view, you'll get overlooked. It's supposed to challenge conventional wisdom. It's supposed to intrigue some and repel others. It's supposed to make people think in new ways. It's supposed to expose something deeper or different than has been seen before.

Remember when I said if you don't craft the narrative, others will make assumptions instead? The assumption might be that you're not worth paying attention to. Diana Vreeland said: *"Most people haven't got a point of view; they need to have it given to them – and what's more, they expect it from you."* It's your responsibility to curate your own brand perspectives so you can reach the right people with them. The bar is higher now, and if you want to be recognised as the authority, people will expect you to provoke their brains in refreshing ways, like a mojito to the cerebrum – extra lime.

Your brand perspectives should be specific to your expertise, industry, clients, and offers. They don't have to be radically different, but you can make them seem so by attaching a unique story to them. Hearing the same message in a different way can be just as powerful as hearing a new message. Put your attention and focus on the people you want to be drawing to you, not the people you're scared of offending, or you fear are going to judge you because of what you say.

What makes a perspective a power perspective? A power perspective is:

1. A fresh take on your industry. A bold or uncommon perspective that challenges conventional wisdom. If it's all been heard before, it won't hold a powerful frequency.
2. A clear stake in the ground. A perspective you feel strongly about and can stand behind. If you waver in your conviction, it won't hold a powerful frequency.

Your power perspectives will build your brand awareness, authority, and affinity. This is the thought leadership aspect and it's what will move people from knowing you to buying from you. My expertise lies in written communication and my work often involves creating messaging for business owners who showcase their value in captivating ways. Your power perspectives *are* your message. You can communicate them in different ways, but the key messages are the power perspectives. Together, these form a unique web of wisdom with a golden thread. A distilled collection of who you are, how you think, why you think it, and how it changes the world. A series of connected thoughts that have the power to position you in a powerful way. This becomes your brand messaging. This becomes what people know you for. (Note that your brand messaging is different from your offer messaging. Offers do need to provide some kind of specific result. It's delivering on your promises within your offers that will instil your reputation as a credible expert.)

THE MYTH OF POLARISATION

"But I don't want to be polarising." This is something I've heard countless times from clients and business owners. Their reasoning? Usually, it's because they don't want to call anyone out – their competitors or their potential clients, for example. They don't want to say any variation of *"You're thinking about this or doing this wrong,"* because who are they to say that and keep their integrity? The reason behind this though is that they don't want to be disagreed with or misunderstood to the point where someone challenges them, vilifies them or, heaven forbid, they're "cancelled". It's this fear that sabotages them from saying the thing they really want to say. Nobody is waiting to hear something they've already heard before. If all anyone ever did was agree with you, they would never buy from you. It's your job to share your unique perspectives, *so you can shift other people's.* You have to challenge people's thinking in order to change their behaviour. Change doesn't come from repeating the same thoughts and behaviours, therefore, personal brands don't become thought leaders by repeating what has been said before.

The hard truth is that somebody will always disagree with you, even if you're Switzerland. If you take a stand for your school of thought, someone will argue for another. If you try to play safe and sit on the fence, someone will criticise you for not having the conviction to take a stand one way or the other. You're not going to move someone emotionally or physically if you sit on the fence. You may think this means you can't win. But this is your opportunity to connect to your power in a new way. If you can't win over everybody, why not try winning over the people who are waiting to hear the exact thing you're not saying?

Polarisation literally means division. The Cambridge Dictionary definition is: *"The fact of people or opinions being divided into two opposing groups."* The idea of division, and therefore intentionally isolating yourself from a group of people, may feel deeply uncomfortable. It's like willingly politicising your brand and, given the state of politics, why would you want to do that? The problem though, is that the reluctance to lean into what polarisation means for you is exactly what will keep you stuck in the epidemic of generic. The power is in the polarisation. If you're not prepared to take a stand for what you do believe in, you're unconsciously taking a stand for something you don't believe in. And you're stopping yourself from helping the exact group of people you have the wisdom to help.

When you think about it that way, polarisation is positive. You're simply making it clear which school of thought you have either pioneered or belong to. The clarity is the conviction. When you can clearly state what you believe and why – even when you know it to be in contrast to another person's belief – the people who you're meant to help will feel safe with you. Being honest in public requires courage that's recognised and respected by those who have been unable to find it elsewhere. It's the feeling of somebody voicing the exact feelings they had previously been unable to articulate. When you can do that, you won't be worried about calling out your competitors. Your attention will be where it's supposed to be – your wisdom and your people.

Let's use a common example of polarisation in entrepreneurship. In the red corner, we have the "hustle and grind" school of thought. This perspective rallies that:

- Hard work is a requirement for great results.
- Rest is overrated.
- When you love what you do, you never work a day in your life.
- Your earnings are attached to how much you work.
- If you don't work whenever you have the time to, you're lazy.

In the blue corner, we have the "relax and prosper" school of thought. This perspective rallies that:

- Working less means earning more.
- Rest is a requirement.
- Work is pointless if you don't enjoy your life.
- Your work has nothing to do with your worth.
- Your ability to be present is more important than productivity.

Even by reading these two simple lists, you will already have a gut feeling as to which school of thought you belong to. Or perhaps, more excitingly, you have a different school of thought – which is exactly how you would start to shape your own power perspectives. Impact is not created by sitting on the fence. You have to be on a field of play. You get to choose the field, the way you play, and whether to change them in the future. Polarisation doesn't require unkindness. You can take a stand for what you believe without tearing down others who believe differently. What do you consider more important? Impacting the one whose life will change as a result of your work? Or avoiding annoying the ninety-nine who were never going to buy from you anyway?

FLAGS OF DEFIANCE AND DEVOTION

Before we get into the power perspectives, we want to decipher your flag of defiance and flag of devotion. For a brand to be positioned in a distinct way, it needs to both stand against and stand for something. This is polarisation in practice. Your flag of defiance represents what you stand strongly against, what you're fighting against, and what you don't believe in. It's the enemy. Imagine you're sticking a flag in the ground and saying, this is what I'm trying to get us away from, are you with me? Your flag of devotion represents what you stand strongly for. What you're fighting for. What you deeply believe in. It's the endgame. Imagine you're sticking a flag in the ground and saying, this is what I want to get us closer to, are you with me? This is how you create your movement, by knowing what you're actually moving from, and what you're moving towards. The movement itself is the how. The plan of attack, if you will. For example, my flag of defiance is the epidemic of generic. I want to rid the world of shallow, same-same, blend-in brands. My flag of devotion is helping people become an irresistible authority with integrity, in a way that respects their personality and capacity. The movement is branding the way you think and everything is pulled together by the golden thread of captivating communication. To help you uncover yours, you can ask yourself these questions.

- Are there any conventional stances in your industry that you completely disagree with or that make you angry?

- What is it about your industry that you want to change?
- Is there anything you wish you could express in your business, but you don't feel comfortable doing so?
- What do you wish you had the audacity to say?
- What do you undeniably believe in with the work you do?
- What most excites you about your business and the work you do in it?
- What's deliberately different about the way you do things in your business?
- What are you willing to / do you do that your competitors can't or won't do?

When you have your answers, these will become integral parts of the brand. They should be considered in all communication decisions.

WHAT DO YOU THINK?

If you want to build a brand around the way you think, you have to actually know what you think, and that requires *thinking* about what you think (stay with me!). Is it really your point of view, or is it what you've heard so many others say? Is it really your point of view, or is it the way it's always been? Is it really your point of view, or have you not considered the alternatives on the table yet? The market is sophisticated, and people aren't interested in regurgitated ideas. They want to know what you *really* think, especially if nobody else is saying it. I've developed a distillation process you can go through to discover what you think and then turn those thoughts into power perspectives. Power perspectives are how you articulate your wisdom with conviction and make it relevant and resonant to your audience. In order to do that, you have to sift through your inner goldmine. You are an incredible, layered, complex human. Trying to put your wisdom into a brand that makes sense to other people is challenging, but when you put in the effort to unlock it, you immediately give yourself a competitive advantage.

This doesn't have to be a long process. But if you want to create depth of connection, shallow thinking isn't going to cut it. Most people don't do this. Consider that an opportunity. As a lawyer, there were two important aspects to my work, critical contemplation and narrative crafting. You couldn't craft a narrative effectively until you'd considered the case from all different angles. You needed to look at all the evidence before forming an opinion about any of it. The more you can uncover new points of view, and the more comfortable you become with the points of view you already have, the easier it will be for you to express them, and the easier it will be for you to connect with the right clients.

1. SHAPE IT

First up. Shape the perspective. You can do this activity with me now if you like. The easiest way to find a perspective to shape? Respond to something. Let your curiosity lead you to something that your mind wants to explore. It could be a client challenge, a piece of work you're doing, an industry trend, a prompt, a piece of content, a line of a book, a TV show, a conversation, an object, or a person. It could be something completely unrelated to the work you do. Once you find something that sparks interest, note your immediate reaction. Why did you find it interesting? What domino effect of thinking did it spur? All you need to do in this stage is shape a line of thought so that if I asked what you were thinking about, you could answer me. Trust your instincts and see where they lead. You could do this in a journal, out loud, in your own head, or with another person. Everyone processes differently. I've always said that I don't write just to share what I think; I write to *discover* what I think. I let my thoughts have thought babies. The key is consciously allowing the thoughts to come without judging them or batting them away. Keep your mind open and record anything that makes you go, *"Ooh, that's an interesting thought."*

Next, develop the perspective with critical contemplation. This is where you sit with and observe your thoughts with discernment. Thinking independently means critically and creatively analysing something from different angles, collecting evidence, asking open questions, and forming your own opinion rather than conforming to one that already exists. The goal here is to go *deeper* or *different* (or both) than what's already established as conventional wisdom in your area of expertise. Deeper: What is something you see being talked about that scratches the surface of the truth? Different: What is something you believe in that nobody else is talking about?

It's essential to separate your expertise from your ego. Question everything. If you have a thought, ask yourself *why* you think it. What influenced that thought? What evidence is there to the contrary? How could you explain that? Apply different lenses. Try a lens that feels uncomfortable. Play in the grey areas. Share your thoughts with someone who can be devil's advocate – for me, that's my husband. He doesn't have an online business, he doesn't do branding, and he works for a large, not-for-profit organisation. His lenses are very different from mine, which means he can see things in ways I can't, and challenge me accordingly. He gets bonus points if he's cooked dinner. You want to end up with a clear point of view that you can stand behind, even if you can't articulate it concisely yet.

2. SHARPEN IT

Once you know what your perspective is, you want to sharpen it. This means giving it a powerful frequency, an edge that cuts through the noise. If thought regurgitation is repeating or repackaging what already exists (and keeps you in the epidemic of generic) then we want to focus on thought refinement or thought fusion. Thought refinement is taking one thought and refining it until it becomes a new thought. (This is a great way to go deeper.) For example, work/life balance is a well-known concept. I took this conventional wisdom and refined it until I had a new way of looking at it. The result was work/life *presence*. It's not about trying to blend work with life, it's about being fully present with either work or life. Thought-fusion is taking more than one thought and fusing them until they become a new thought. (This is a great way to get something different.)

Ideally, you want to condense a perspective into one or two strong sentences that can be supported with context. You're basically putting your thoughts through a distillation process so that what people experience is the most potent version. Great communication is about complex ideas made simple. Everything is nuanced, and yet we can't always communicate that nuance, or people don't have time to absorb it. How can you communicate your perspective with power in just a few words or sentences? Depth can still be found there.

Let's look at some examples. In my world, I'm surrounded by people selling messaging formulas (like the "I help" statement) and content templates. These have always felt forced to me. I love a good framework, but I believe formulas and templates deprive the world of creative expression. It's a form of putting yourself in a box, and once you're in there, you start to rely on it for support. (Do you see how this perspective gives you a sense of who I am as a person?) When I looked at these thoughts, I asked myself: What's the strongest way of communicating this in just one breath? If people could only remember one thought, what would I want it to be? How can I say this in a way that clearly shows what I stand for or against? That's how I created the power perspective: Thought leaders don't rely on templates.

Let's look at some other examples. Claire Sweet is a finance expert, and she shares all sorts of interesting strategies on how to make the most of your money and turn it into lasting wealth.

Power perspective: Poor people use debit cards. Rich people use credit cards.

Context: Not having at least one credit card is damaging your ability to build wealth and could leave you financially exposed.

If you read that perspective, depending on your circumstances, you could get your feathers in a right ruffle. The context is important. That's where nuance is. The power perspective acts as a strong hook, a pattern interrupt, and opens up a gap of intrigue. It has a powerful frequency. The context provides the nuance. Together, they form a piece of the brand narrative. Claire could have said: It's smart to use a credit card even when you have cash reserves. But do you feel how much less powerful that is to read? This is why it's imperative that you shape and sharpen your perspectives before you share them if you want to maximise their impact.

What if your vibe isn't so bold or forthright? Power can be infused and communicated in different ways. It could be a soft power, an inspiring power, a comedic power, or a kind power. None of these are antonyms for strong.

Ashley Beaudin is the Gentle Business Coach, and she supports business owners to do their most meaningful work in a way that honours their nervous system.

Power perspective: I think we romanticise quick transformations because they feel easier to sell, but rarely do they bring about the kind of growth our hearts are yearning for.

Context: In a world of "change your life in ninety days" and handy to-do lists, it takes courage to practice presence and consider what it could look like for our businesses to facilitate the slow, steady transformation of the soul.

This is a beautiful example of how to curate a deeply resonant presence. This kind of power perspective challenges the status quo and helps Ashley's people feel *so seen*. The power is not just in the perspective, it's in how that makes people feel when they receive it. It's like a giant exhale to realise that you don't have to think or act in conventional ways. It's gentle in the way it's written, but Ashley even states: *"Do not confuse my gentleness for a lack of power, sovereignty, or conviction."*

3. SHARE IT

Finally, we of course have to share our power perspective. You can have the most powerful message on the planet, but it means nothing if the only head it spends time in is your own. This isn't a fact you have to prove in court; it's *your* truth. Sharing requires courage, conviction, and context. You need to be brave enough to say what you *really* think, with no dilution to appease those whom the message isn't meant for. You need to stand behind your perspective *and* stay open to having it shifted. And you need to be able to provide context so that people understand the real meaning behind the message you are communicating to them.

It's only through sharing your power perspectives that you can gauge their impact. And that means sharing them a *lot* more than once. You'll know they're hitting the sweet spot when dream clients start to repeat them back to you, competitors start mimicking you, your demand increases, new opportunities land in your lap, and you feel like powerfully expressing yourself is the only piece that's been missing all along. The more you share, the more you'll want to share. And the more you want to share, the greater the outcome for everyone.

YOU'RE ALLOWED TO CHANGE YOUR MIND

Another concern I often hear is: *"What if I change my mind?"* as if that's not part of normal human evolution. If you went through your adult years and *didn't* change your mind, I'd be concerned for your self-awareness. You can change your perspectives without changing your personality or philosophies. And there is a big difference between changing your mind and being able to stand behind your reasons for it and sharing a thought you don't believe in anymore. I would have far more respect for the person who said, look I've changed my mind and here's why, compared to the person who refused to be open and humble enough to change their mind. That would tell me they're more concerned with their ego than their impact. Growth doesn't happen without critical thinking. Conviction isn't about staying true to everything you've ever said, it's about staying true to the person you evolve into. Because your thoughts will evolve with you. Just like feelings come and go, thoughts can too. We're not married to our thinking. But we do have a responsibility to provide context for why we think the way we think. If you're not open to changing your mind, you may miss opportunities that are meant for you.

Researcher Adam Grant talks about the importance of *rethinking*. When you become so devoted to what you're doing, and you see success from it, it's easy to put blinkers on to the real world around you. Why do you think Blockbuster went out of business? Because they couldn't rethink their position in the market. They didn't believe people would ever buy movies online, so they turned down a deal from Netflix. Look where we are today. Who do you know who uses a Blackberry? Nobody, because they couldn't rethink their position in the market. They didn't believe touchscreen phones would replace their keypad. Both of these companies rented / sold goods, but when your perspective *is* the product, rethinking is imperative to stay relevant in a market that changes like the wind.

ACTIONS

- Identify a golden thread you can pull through your answers to questions so far (it's okay if this doesn't feel clear yet).
- Decide your flags of defiance and devotion.
- Shape, sharpen, and share a small selection of power perspectives.

PHASE 2: EXTRACT YOUR EDGE

Would you drop £10k+ for someone to write one or two words for you? Did you just guffaw? Well, that's exactly what Alexandra Watkins does. She owns a business and product naming company called Eat My Words (obviously her own name had to be 5*) and her signature services *start* at £10k for a two-week turnaround. How can she charge this kind of a premium and still be so in demand? Because she's made herself the irresistible authority. She's worked with hundreds of brands (my favourite is a frozen yoghurt called Spoon Me), has a book called *My Name is Awesome,* a course, she's a speaker, and she *only does naming*. Naming is what she does. But everything about her brand is showing us how she thinks. Lots of companies create brand and product names, but none of them think like Alexandra and this is what gives her an edge that sears through the competition.

Alongside making her expert perspectives abundantly clear, she's developed a catchy proprietary framework called

SMILE & SCRATCH. These are acronyms for the five qualities every great brand name has, and the seven deal breakers, and she uses this to both serve and teach. This is her intellectual property. It's what she's become known for beyond the names she creates and how she's diversified her business model. She uses a creative concept linked to her own brand name to communicate in a unique and memorable way. For example, she has lines like: *"Our names bring home the bacon"* and *"Brand names that consumers eat up"* throughout her website. Her tone of voice is quirky and playful – which suggests the approach she takes to her work – and instils trust that you'll get a name that makes you smile (see above acronym). She has a name evaluation test on her website that lets people see how strong their brand or product name is, and this introduces them to her framework. She drops globally recognised client names like a whole sack of hot potatoes. I could go on.

Once you've explored your brain and shaped some power perspectives, then it's time to move to the next phase.

PHASE 2 OF THE WISDOMBRANDING FRAMEWORK: EXTRACT YOUR EDGE

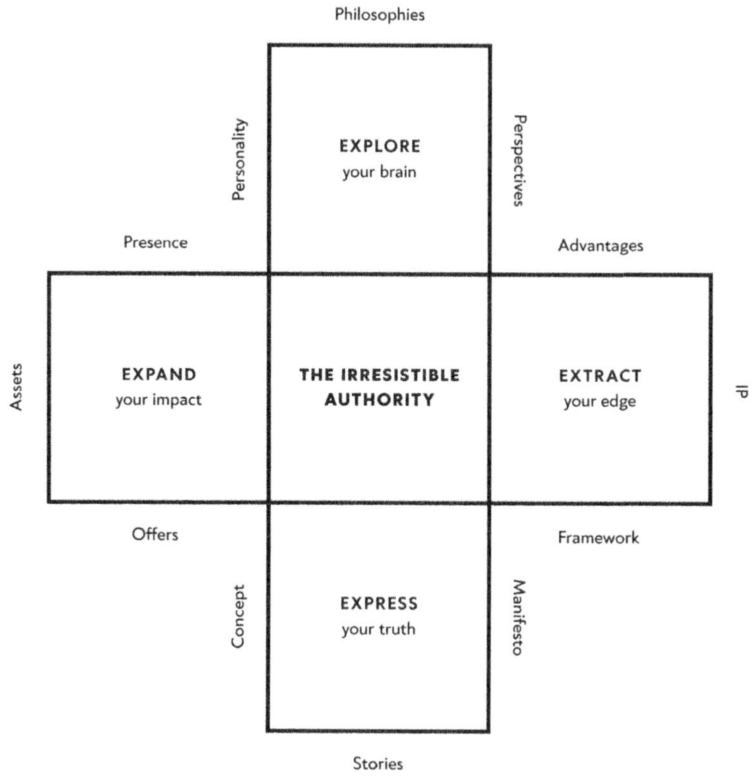

Advantages: Translate your unique essence, expertise, and experience into reasons why people want to work with you above anybody else.

IP: Turn your most valuable ideas into irresistible and uncopyable concepts that allow people to understand how your brilliance can help them.

Framework: Structure your intuitive approach to what you do in a simple yet potent proprietary model that helps you instantly elevate your positioning.

Core phase outcome: proprietary framework.

Extracting your edge is not about trying to be edgy. It's intentionally sifting through and chiselling away at everything that you are until you're left with something sharp enough to make the competition irrelevant. The sharper your edge, the deeper the difference you make.

8

ADVANTAGES

What's your unique differentiator? This is a common question, and yet it's almost impossible to answer unless your service or product is truly pioneering. Sometimes it is. Usually, it isn't. This is another reason why the epidemic of generic exists. It can feel like a case of who can shout the loudest rather than who is the best choice. What you do will seldom be snowflake-level unique, but the *way* you do it and the way you *think* about it will be. The way your brain works is your point of difference. Build a brand around that. Rather than trying to find one specific thing that makes you uniquely different, which *will* feel like trying to lie yourself down in a tiny box that eventually stifles you, focus on a collection of things that together make you your own competitive advantage. You get to build your own box. And then expand it as you go… or rebuild it when you outgrow it.

Now that you've explored your brain and gained some direction on who you are and how you think, you next want to extract your edge. In the Cambridge Dictionary, edge is defined as *having an advantage over other people.* The point of extracting your edge is not (just) to differentiate yourself, it's to demonstrate your advantage. It's not just how are you different, it's *why that matters.* It's important to know what's happening in your market, but rather than focusing all your attention on how to be different from your competitors, I recommend looking at how you're similar to the people you'd most like to work with, and what kinds of advantages will help build intrigue, rapport, and trust in them. You may find that doing the latter automatically differentiates you.

Your edge is supposed to be sharp. It won't cut through the competition otherwise. You don't have to be loud out on these internet streets, but you do need to be sharp. Your edge is what people will come to recognise about you, and it's what will help you become The One versus one of many. Your deliberate advantages have to make sense in the context of what you do. Me being a lawyer is a differentiator in the sense that many people who deliver the kinds of services I do haven't been lawyers, but that puts the focus on my competitors and not my clients. In that context, it isn't relevant. But when I shift the focus to how my being a former lawyer elevates the perception my best-fit clients have of me and demonstrates that I can help them in ways others can't, you get:

- I know how to craft a compelling narrative.
- I'm trained in critical thinking.
- It was my job to be a clear communicator.
- I have a 100% track record as an advocate.
- I was literally paid to think and advise.
- I know what it's like to perform in a high-pressure environment.

- I have a high standard of education which gives me a baseline level of intellectual credibility.

For some people, this information may not draw them closer to me. That's fine. But for the right people, when you then layer this on top of other advantages, you start to build a strong case for *why you*.

THE NICHE CAKE

You don't need to find your niche. You need to own your edge. When I started my business, I had no idea I was also becoming a personal brand. I was simply using my skills to offer a service to people who would pay me. There's no problem with that, certainly not in those earlier years of business. But when I reduced my identity to that of a skilled service provider, I didn't give people a good enough reason to choose me over another skilled service provider. Why should they choose me, especially if the other person is cheaper? The Cambridge Dictionary defines a niche as: *"A job or position that is very suitable for someone, especially one that they like."* We're thinking about this in terms of business ownership, so let's remove job from this description. If a niche is just finding a suitable and likeable position, why does it cause business owners so much mental strife? First, it automatically suggests competition. We niche not just to find a place for ourselves, but to find a place that isn't already occupied. Tough in a seemingly saturated and sophisticated online world. Secondly, some people struggle to choose a niche because they think they can't fit their multi-passionate selves into it.

People aren't paying you for what you're passionate about. They're paying for your mind. If you can't show how your expertise is relevant, you will automatically make it more difficult for anyone to buy from you. That's why I believe in focusing your brand around the way you think, and then having your personality and passions act as context. Besides, you're not married to a niche. If you really want to, shift it. Just not every month.

You're likely an established business owner. You've probably got a niche, want to pivot your niche, already change your niche too often, or recoil at the idea of niching. There's so much to argue about over niching – and not just how to pronounce it. Should you niche? If yes, how? How narrow do you go? What if you change your mind? If not, how are people supposed to understand what you do? For me, the topic of niching is, like basically everything on this earth, nuanced. Here are some perspectives I have about niching:

- It's helpful when you're starting out and you haven't yet solidified a reputation.
- Choosing a niche can help you decide what you do and don't enjoy.
- A narrow niche can provide the greatest opportunities.
- You are not the niche; you are a layer of it.
- Even when you think you don't have a niche, you do.
- Evolving your niche is completely normal as your expertise, market, results, and perspectives evolve.

I don't believe it's a case of having a niche, not having a niche, or the niche simply being you. It's more of a layered cake that you can audit accordingly. If you're trying to differentiate yourself in some way, you do want to give consideration to your niche, but you want to give more consideration to your narrative. How do you translate your wisdom in a way that demonstrates your competitive advantages? That's what will give you an edge. The reason why people don't like to niche themselves, or at least not too narrowly, is because it feels like an immediate pressure on their chest. It's suffocating to the soul which has so much to give, to so many, in different ways.

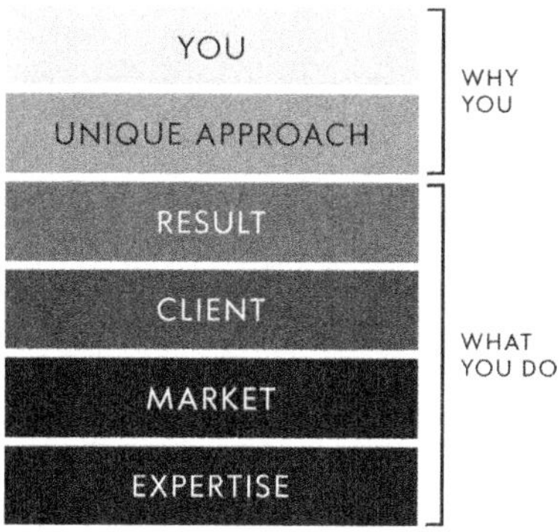

You: your personality, philosophies, and perspectives.

Unique approach: the special way you facilitate that result.

Result: what you provide to/the problem you solve for the client.

Client: the particular person within that market.

Market: the place where your expertise is relevant.

Expertise: the skills you bring to the table.

Let's look at a partial example of my niche.

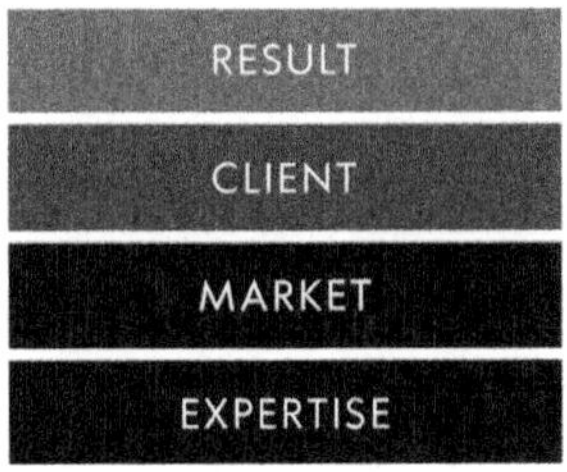

Result: become the irresistible authority.

Client: established consultants, coaches, and creative service providers who want to elevate their positioning using thought leadership.

Market: online business owners.

Expertise: brand positioning and messaging.

This is where many stop – and it's why they stay in the epidemic of generic. Competition lives here too. When I reference branding what you do, this is what I mean. It's about making a person a promise based on your knowledge and expertise. This can serve you well, but this is only four layers of the cake. These are the *what you do* layers. The layers that demonstrate relevance. We still need to address the *why you* layers. The layers that provoke resonance. This is where competition starts to significantly decrease. Consider this the icing and cherry on top. The cake can exist without them, but it won't taste nearly as good.

Here are the remaining layers of my niche cake:

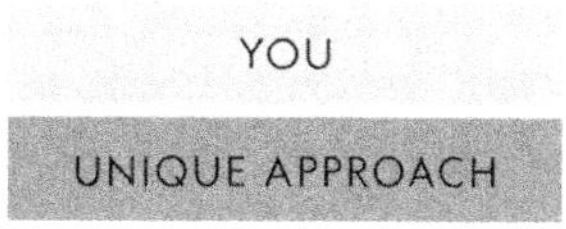

You: when you brand what you do, there will always be competition, but when you brand the way you think, competition becomes irrelevant.

Unique approach: WisdomBranding.

While you ideally want to have an answer for each layer of the pyramid, if you're super narrow in one or two areas, you don't have to be narrow in all the others. For example, an unusual skill doesn't *need* a super-niche market or client. One of my former clients, Alyea Sandevar, is a gamification expert. Because her expertise itself is so niche, she doesn't have to go narrow in other areas (unless she wants to).

STRENGTH STACKING

Ronda Rousey was a UFC champion, undefeated for twelve professional fights, and seemingly untouchable. *She had serious skills.* She was also the first woman to join the franchise. *She had a fascinating story.* In the ring, she grappled like nobody else. *She had a superpower.* So, how did she go from being the UFC golden girl to being knocked out by a relative newcomer? Instead of focusing on her biggest strength, grappling, Rousey wanted to show the world she could win with her weakness, striking. She didn't. She lost her belt, her undefeated record, and unfortunately, her sense of self for a long time afterwards. The person who beat her was a kickboxing specialist. How did she win? *A kick.*

When we think about our competitive advantages, what we're really doing is stacking our skills, story, and superpowers in a way that's relevant and resonant. Too many business owners try to win with their weaknesses when they could lean in and leverage their strength stack. As your wisdom evolves, your advantages will too, and it's normal to feel like you've reached a point where you've outgrown your audience and offers. It doesn't mean burning everything to the ground. Look at your stack in a new way, consider what purpose is driving you, and see the opportunities that open up. Your strength stack will only grow. So long as you can effectively communicate your advantages, you'll be able to make your competition irrelevant. It goes without saying that to be seen as an authority you have to actually *be* an authority, at least, in my world you do. (No cults were built in the writing of this book.) If you want to claim expertise in an area you aren't an actual expert in, you'll end up building the wrong kind of reputation. Here's what your audience will be wondering:

Skills: What are you brilliant at (and how can that help me)?

Story: What have you been through (and how does that speak to my identity)?

Superpowers: What's unusually strong and special about you (and why should I care)?

To answer these questions, consider everything that's made you who you are and got you to where you are today – life responsibilities, roles, jobs, failures, achievements, experience, clients, results, etc.

- Where have you reached mastery?
- What are you surprisingly great at?
- What challenges have you overcome?
- Why do you do what you do?
- What specific moment in time put you on the path you're on now (turning point)?
- What could you bang on about for hours?
- What do you always get complimented on?
- When do you feel at your most powerful? Why?
- What is your zone of excellence?
- What is your zone of genius?
- What do you do better than everybody else?
- What do you perceive to be a weakness that could actually be a strength?
- What does the market need most and how are you uniquely able to fulfil that need?

Consider the crossovers between life and business. For example, I'm a parent to a toddler. Sometimes, he has big emotions and he's developmentally incapable of handling them on his own. My job as the parent is to stay calm and keep myself regulated so he's able to do the same. My experience shows I have incredible patience! How could this be a relevant superpower in my business? It means I can create a safe-as-possible space for clients to work through the often-messy process of building a brand that helps them become the irresistible authority. Clients have reflected how patient I am with them as they work through their challenges and that I'm a breath of fresh air in a world of people who push, force, and lose patience when progress isn't being made faster.

When you start to unpack and stack your skills, story, and superpowers, ask yourself how they're relevant to the person you want to reach through your brand. You're not stacking *everything* that makes you brilliant. Your skills must be helpful to them. Your story must allow them to see parts of themselves in it. Your superpowers must be of value.

TRUST TRIGGERS

Hands up if you've heard of the know, like, trust factor. Okay, put your hand down. This has become a polarising concept itself, but if people don't know you, they obviously won't buy from you. If they don't like you, they may buy from you, but it could be a subpar experience. If they don't trust you, they'd be taking a risk to buy from you. We *want* people to trust us, and we ideally want them to like us too. People don't *just* buy from people who promise them something they want; they buy from humans they like. People need to trust you, but it goes deeper than that. People need to *trust themselves* in your presence.

So how do you make someone trust you? If you're a trustworthy person, this won't feel like a challenge, but it's one thing to get people to trust you, and another to get them to trust you'll get them results. Trust is built through a collection of factors, such as connection, compassion, and communication, but one of the biggest is credibility. The more credible you are, the easier it will be for people will trust you. They will *believe* what you say with less hesitation. A trust trigger is a simple signal to your best-fit client that you're a safe bet. For example:

- You have a certain qualification.
- You've helped a number of clients like them reach the result they want.

- You're a pioneer in your industry.
- You have strong social proof.
- You're endorsed by another credible person.

The "places I've been featured" logo bar you often see on people's websites is an example of a trust trigger. These triggers compound, so if you consistently infuse them throughout your brand experience, you'll deepen the trust automatically over time.

You've heard about touchpoints – the number of times someone has to experience you before they buy from you. How many touchpoints on average does it take for someone to buy? Google tells me eight, though I'm sure I've heard as high as 27. When your attention is so in demand, making any kind of choice becomes more difficult. That is the choice paradox. When you're presented with so many options, you have to work harder to believe you're choosing the "right" one. And sometimes, it's easier not to make a choice at all. This is another reason why building a brand around what you do, especially when you're in a noisy market, means you'll have to work harder to become the irresistible authority.

Touchpoints in and of themselves don't equal trust. Your touchpoints have to be genuine and of high quality. They are, of course, about what you say (in content, an ad, on a call, etc.), but they're also about how you make a person feel – understood, safe, and confident. It's the compound effect of high-quality touchpoints that build trust. These days, trust isn't assumed; it has to be earned and you can earn it faster by combining trust triggers with your competitive advantages (skills, story, superpowers) and sprinkling them through your communications.

Here are a few of my trust triggers to give you a starting point:

- High % of clients have worked with me multiple times (shows loyalty and reputation).
- Nine+ years in the online industry (shows staying power).
- Learned from some of the best teachers in the world on branding and copywriting (shows commitment to mastery).
- Have worked with hundreds of clients (shows depth of expertise and experience).
- Former lawyer (shows a level of intellect).
- Have worked with five, six, seven, and even eight-figure clients (shows credibility).
- Have supported clients to achieve results including 1000% ROI, a £350,000 launch, best revenue months ever, booking out their premium services with dream clients, having strangers sign packages purely because of the power of their brand and website, and so much more (shows capability).

ACTIONS

- Build your niche cake.
- Highlight your three most valuable skills.
- Find the main "turning point" in your origin story.
- Select your greatest superpowers (surprising things you do better than anyone else).
- Collect your trust triggers.

9

IP

Elizabeth Gilbert had an idea. Her next book was going to be about a character going to the Amazon. She spent hours conceptualising the book but hadn't actually begun writing it when she met another author called Ann Patchett. In a casual conversation between the two, it transpired that Ann had already written a book about a woman going to the Amazon. There were so many synchronicities between the ideas that Elizabeth could hardly believe it. In her book, *Big Magic*, she describes this experience and suggests that ideas search for receptive minds to bring them into existence. If an idea isn't made manifest through one mind, it will search for another. If two people have similar ideas, it doesn't necessarily mean one has copied the other. They could simply have been on the same creative wavelength.

So, what's the difference between an idea and intellectual property? Ownership. Intellectual property (IP) is a creation of the mind. It includes names, inventions, designs, writing, etc. You can't own an idea if you keep it locked in your head.

Have you ever had a genius idea, got excited about it, promised yourself you would share it when you had the time to properly formulate it, and then a few days, weeks, or months down the line, seen someone else talking about the exact same thing? And your initial reaction is: *They stole my idea.* It might feel like that, and you have permission to kick yourself, but it's not your idea if you don't claim ownership of it through creation. A mere idea isn't valuable unless it exists outside the mind. Some IP protection is awarded automatically (typically, in online expertise-based businesses, that's copyright, which is applied to anything you write), and some protection you have to apply for (typically, in online expertise-based businesses, that's trademarks). In the UK, trademarks are applied for in categories and they have to be distinct enough to be accepted, for example, I once applied for the mark "Storymarketing" and it was rejected because it wasn't deemed distinct enough. The Captivation Code® was.

As a thought leader with an expertise-based online business, you're monetising your mind. You're adding power perspectives to the industry and creating concepts to help translate your ideas in ways that move people closer to a result they want. Concepts are a way of making what could be a commodity into something more unique and interesting. When you create a concept, you're giving an idea an identity. You're showing people how you think beyond a thought itself. For example, power perspectives is a teaching concept. It's an idea that I break down using the "shape, sharpen, share" framework that shows you how to generate your own power perspectives. Other concepts within my business include:

- Storymarketing Matrix (the approach I take to sharing stories in your business).
- Wisdombox (my proprietary framework model).
- Flags of defiance and devotion.

You can build materials, resources, curriculums, and more from your ideas. These are all a result of the unique way your expertise and perspectives help people get a result. This is your intellectual property. What's something you repeatedly teach that you have a unique approach to? What's a question you always get asked and people are always surprised by the answer? What do you get most excited to talk about that nobody else seems to talk about like you do? These kinds of questions can help you discover where your most valuable ideas are. Dangerous ideas disrupt and activate. Simple ideas relieve and excite. Both require courage. Danger requires you to dare to create what others are scared to. Simplicity requires you to challenge the complexity of what others have already created. This is an opportunity for you to flex your mind and challenge it to go deeper or different.

STEAL LIKE AN ARTIST

"For us, that crossed an ethical line." I felt sick when I read that in my inbox a few years ago. It's possibly the most horrible thing a person who always strives to act with integrity can hear. I was blacklisted from a branding program, without notice and without a refund, because I suggested I might like to create my own program in the future. It was a great lesson in how not to treat your clients. And what shocked me most was how incongruent their behind-the-scenes behaviour was with their public persona. Just because you have *expertise and experience* in an area doesn't mean you own it. These people

did not create and own the topic of branding. They developed their own perspectives and teaching concepts within it. The value isn't in the expertise, it's in how you think about it and how it manifests through you.

This experience gave me some "little t" trauma. Trying to be unique has been the biggest bottleneck to my success, which is borderline ridiculous given that this book is about leveraging your unique wisdom. When you try too hard to be different, you may miss the gifts that are right in front of your face and miss using them to help people. One of the biggest reasons people don't leverage their brain's brilliance more is because they think it's not brilliant enough already, exactly as it is. They think an idea, perspective, concept, or message has to be never-seen-before revolutionary for it to be considered "worthy" of showing up with, building a brand around, and communicating in different ways. This simply isn't true.

Steal Like An Artist is a fun and fabulous book by Austin Kleon. The point the book makes is that nothing is truly original, and all creative work builds on work that already exists. Where do you think inspiration comes from? It's rarely your butthole. It comes from what you're influenced by. And if you consciously choose to be influenced by other people's existing art, you can create fresh art from it. Combining existing ideas is what creates new ones. I know my best ideas are a fusion of the brilliant minds I learn from and the collection of lenses I use to look at the world. Once you've collected enough information and ideas from other people, your own will pop up out of nowhere, ready to be birthed through you. There's a reason why you get your best ideas when out for a walk, in the shower, or while tossing and turning at midnight. If you want to have influential ideas, allow yourself to be influenced by other ideas.

Do you want to be a leader? It's okay to be a follower too. We can only lead with our own ideas once we've been a follower of other people's. We need awareness of what already exists so that we can apply our own lenses and create something new in a space where we co-exist with other leaders wearing their own lenses.

THE TRIPLE THREAT TEST

You can't be perceived as the must-have in your market unless you position yourself that way. Your brain is the asset. What makes an idea worth branding? When it's specific, sticky, and stampable, like a fingerprint. This is where we can start to develop *uniquely on-brand* mental associations. Put your own ideas through the triple threat test:

Specific: Clearly defined and identifiable as your own.

Sticky: Memorable. An idea worth retaining.

Stampable: A repeatable constant. If you want to become known for your ideas, you need to stamp them all over the place.

Let's look at a product example. Consider the global fashion brand Christian Louboutin. They sell shoes, like many other brands, but their "fingerprint" is the red sole. The brand has become synonymous with it. It's specific (red sole), sticky (easy to recognise, and no other brand is allowed to use it), and stampable (it features on all their shoes). When you have the fingerprint, you can support it with context. Christian Louboutin, the creator of the red sole, believed red wasn't just a colour, it was an attitude. The women who wear them embody that, so, the idea speaks to the *identity* of the buyer. Louboutin has firmly established itself in the high-end, luxury market and that fingerprint has built them a reputation based on exclusivity and desire. It's allowed them to expand and evolve with time into gorgeously packaged lipsticks, for example, which cost a lot more than the average lipstick! They can do that and charge premium prices because they've branded and positioned themselves accordingly using a simple idea.

What big ideas do you have that could become "brand fingerprints" that make you effortlessly stand out in an epidemic of generic? Over time, the more you express them, the more they will become associated with you without people even having to think about it.

ACTIONS

- Put one of your big ideas through the triple threat test (specific, sticky, stampable).

10

FRAMEWORK

The Cambridge Dictionary defines a framework as: *"A system of rules, ideas, or beliefs that is used to plan or decide something."* In the context of personal branding, a framework enables you to communicate the foundations of how you think in a simplified and structured way that helps the right people understand what's important to you and how you will support them to get a result. If you google "positioning framework" or "positioning model", you'll get various ideas for how to use visual structures to understand what your brand positioning is. This can be helpful, but when you're the face of the brand, a framework, or even a collection of "mental models" that visually demonstrate the way you think, can be used as a positioning *tool*. The framework itself can shape the perception of your brand in the minds of your ideal clients and help them choose you over somebody else offering a similar result. A framework allows you to codify your genius. It's the zoomed-out system for how you approach your work and get people results. You can then zoom in on the individual sections for context and outcomes.

Having a framework goes far beyond being a positioning tool, though. It forms the backbone of your entire brand. Want a simple way to translate your wisdom to an ideal client? Look at your framework for guidance. Wondering what content to create? Look at your framework for guidance. Considering creating an authority asset like a podcast or keynote? Look at your framework for guidance. Want to create a curriculum for a course or program? Look at your framework for guidance. This book is literally a breakdown of my WisdomBranding framework!

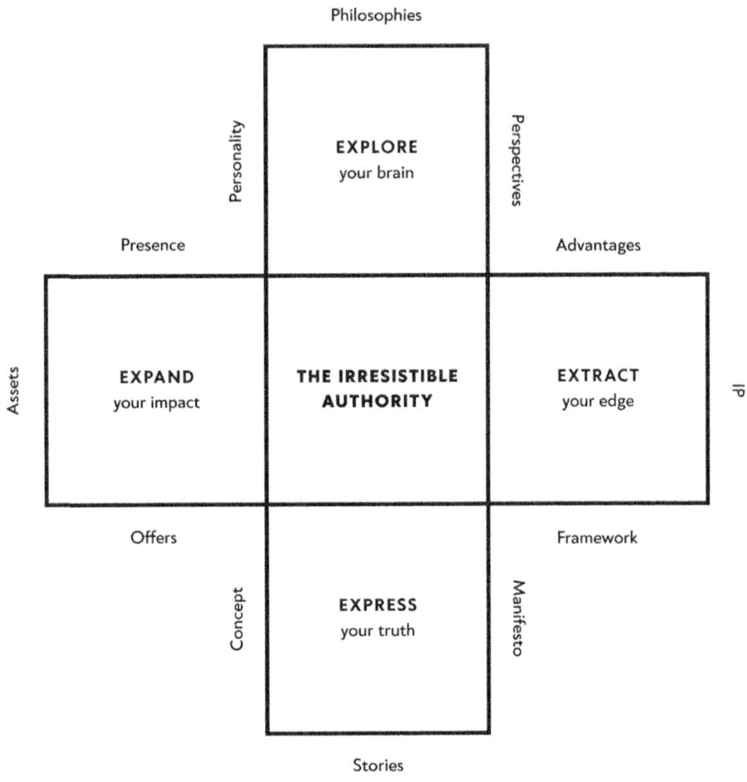

If you've ever felt like you don't want to be boxed into a brand, and it's impossible to imagine being known for one thing when there are so many things you love talking about, having a proprietary framework can provide a structure that allows for creative flow. Because the whole point is to give a zoomed-out view. You have free rein for how you zoom in. And just like power perspectives, you can iterate your framework over time. The more people you work with, the more wisdom you'll develop.

CODIFYING YOUR GENIUS

Crystallising your wisdom into a framework is a way of simplifying the complex and bringing visibility to the intangible, but when you have so much gold in your mind, translating it into a snapshot graphic that communicates the essence of that gold can be exceptionally difficult. This is where it helps to have a positioning expert (like me) or an instructional designer to act as your mirror and reflect back the most powerful parts of your gifts, advantages, approach, and the way you think about the work you do. As an expert, you'll likely work intuitively, especially if you're creative. What's unique about it won't necessarily be obvious to you, and you may even feel like you don't have a special way of thinking or signature approach to the work you do. That's simply not true. It's just hard to see the label when you're inside the jar.

When you have a framework, you also have a foundation for scaling, if that's something you want to do. Rather than customising your genius for every client you work with, a framework helps you *codify* your genius so it can be applied and adapted to multiple people at the same time. Your framework *could* be a linear step-by-step process, but it doesn't have to be. A framework shows people the way you think; a process shows them what to do. Your core framework can be supported by other mental models. These could be built out from your perspectives, processes, and teaching concepts. For example, my core framework is the WisdomBranding framework which I'm walking you through in this book. I then also have other models for parts of what I teach, like the niche cake and the brand authority profiles, and many others in my Google Doc drafts!

There are six types of frameworks I'm going to talk through in this book. You don't have to limit yourself to one, but I'd strongly recommend you focus on creating one that really forms the backbone of your work and the way you think about it. This gives you a foundation to build your expression on, with supportive power perspectives, stories, and outcomes.

TRIANGLE

The triangle is one of the simplest frameworks to work with and it can be applied to almost anything. There are various ways you could develop your triangular framework. Here are some ideas.

Phases

The centre of the triangle could represent a desired identity or result. Then the three points or sides of the triangle represent three phases people go through in order to reach the result. One of my former clients, Heather Clunie, is a therapist, and after exploring her brain we discovered that her golden thread was "connection" in three key areas. The self, other people, and the environment. We created a triangular framework and built out her signature offer from there. Each point of the triangle had its own set of perspectives and outcomes.

Challenges/outcomes

Alternative ways of looking at the triangle are that each of the points represents a challenge to overcome before a result is achieved, or three smaller outcomes.

Philosophies/perspectives

Another one of my former clients, Tiffany Williams, is a kitchen and bathroom designer, and we developed a simple framework for her based on her design philosophy: function, flow, and finesse. Each point had its own explanation (the context) that helped her audience understand why this was her approach – and why they should choose her.

The triangle is a great choice if you've never developed a framework before and you want to keep things simple.

VENN

The Venn diagram is a common way to create a visual model because it has so much flexibility. While the triangle has three distinct points, the Venn puts unique characteristics in circles and shared characteristics in overlapping spaces. This helps provide further context within the visual itself. You can use two, three, or four circles – you could use even more but I wouldn't recommend that because it gets confusing.

ACRONYM

Acronyms are ideal if you want people to have a particular mental association, even if they don't recall the details. Remember Alexandra Watkins of Eat My Words? She uses the acronym SMILE – five qualities needed for a winning name. This is the approach she takes herself when developing names, and it's also what she teaches in her course and book. She also has the acronym SCRATCH which represents the seven dealbreakers that will harm your name and repel customers.

One of my clients, evergreen scaling strategist Polly Lavarello, created an acronym framework using her brand positioning concept of CUSHY business.

ARCHETYPES

An archetype is a typical identity of something. Depending on how you're labelled, it means you'll possess certain characteristics or show certain patterns. The hero and the villain are common archetypes in films and books. Hero equals good, must be the saviour. Villain equals bad, must be stopped. Archetypes are a powerful positioning tool because the identity you give someone will create mental associations. They will immediately relate the result to their reality. One of my clients, Natasha Leigh Bray, is a true pioneer in the therapy and healing industry, and she's an incredible example of the power of leveraging IP as a personal brand. She created her version of archetypes, called Success Saboteur Archetypes®. People can take a quiz to discover their biggest saboteur, and each one forms a piece of the curriculum for her signature program.

- The Hustler
- The Outcast
- The Overgiver
- The Imposter
- The Overprotector

Other examples of well-known archetypes include Sally Hogshead's Fascination Advantages and Roger James Hamilton's Wealth Dynamics.

THE GENIUS MODEL®

The Genius Model®, created by Simon Bowen, is similar to the Venn diagram in the way it looks, but it has a clear focus. The foundation of the model is that the customer/client is at the heart. The three main circles that overlap represent three things the customer wants. Then around the edge are nine things you as the brand do better than anyone else. It's a way of ensuring that the client's desires are centred (literally) and that the brand is of service to those desires.

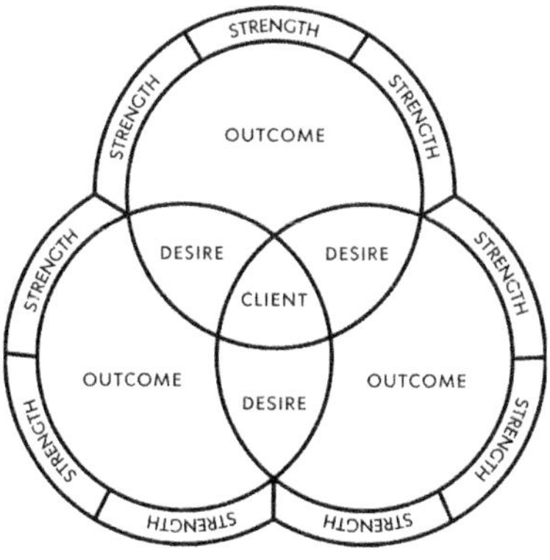

WISDOMBOX

The WisdomBox is a framework I developed, and that I use for my own framework. So meta. Here it is again.

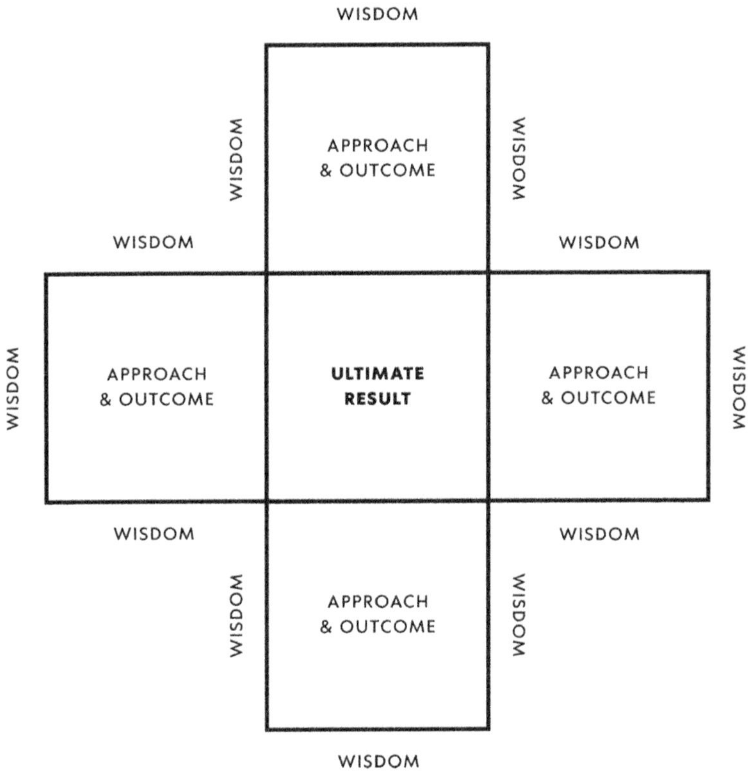

I describe this as unboxing your wisdom. It's your unique way of thinking and working unwrapped. Like with the Genius Model®, the desired identity or ultimate result for the client is at the centre. This is the sweet spot between what your dream clients want and how you want to help them get it. There are then four phases, principles, or pillars, each with three sub-categories and one core outcome, that together facilitate the ultimate result.

With this approach, you're not squeezing yourself into a box that already exists, you're building your own. This breathes, expands, and evolves as you and your dream client do.

ACTIONS

- Draft your proprietary framework using one of the example models.

PHASE 3: EXPRESS YOUR TRUTH

Here's the part where we create your client avatar. *Kidding.* You say you don't want to fit into a box, but that's what you think you need to do with your clients by creating an avatar for them? No. Avatars are overrated and unnecessary when you're grounded in your power perspectives. When you're connected with your wisdom and can articulate it with conviction, the right people will listen. Most people start with who their ideal client is and then shape their brand to fit, which is why many of them don't feel at home within their own brand. It's the ultimate people-pleasing move. They've built it to please the person they want to work with, rather than building it to please themselves and trusting it will translate perfectly to the person they want to work with. Yes, it's important to know who you're here to help, the challenges they face, the fears they have, and the desires that drive them, but if you make the brand all about them, you risk losing yourself.

Have you ever obsessed about speaking the language of your ideal client? Sure, we all have, because that's what we've been taught to do – get inside their head, extract their problems and desires in their own words, and turn them into marketing messages. I, too, have taught this. I called it being a "thought thief" (though the reasons we buy go far deeper than our conscious thoughts). And I'm not saying you shouldn't do this. It's highly effective, hence why it's a universal principle of copywriting. The problem is that your competitors can do that too. So, while you might be unique, your client's problems, fears, desires, and dreams aren't, which means you *do* have competitors, and if you want to be heard (and chosen) over them, you need to be using language that they aren't.

Messaging is a delicate dance between what you want to say and what they need to hear. Focus too much on what you want to say, it may miss the mark with your market, but focus too much on what you think they need to hear and you risk blending into the epidemic of generic and even losing your identity in the process of trying to be heard (and chosen). The way to make sure you're doing both is to consider relevance and resonance. Relevance is the authoritative context. Resonance is the emotional context. Relevance builds demand, resonance stokes desire. If you want to intentionally become a person of interest, share your wisdom in ways that cover both bases. Ask yourself:

- Does this communication connect with a challenge or unmet need my audience has, and does it make it obvious that I can help with that?
- Does this communication make my reader feel seen, heard, and understood?

You want to identify with your ideal clients on an emotional level. This isn't just about the problems they have or the results they want – that's where your offer messaging will come in. This is about getting to the core of who they are as a human and showing them that *you get them*. That they are not only safe with you but meant for you.

Once you've extracted your edge and crafted your proprietary framework, it's time to get creative about communicating your voice and viewpoints.

PHASE 3 OF THE WISDOMBRANDING FRAMEWORK: EXPRESS YOUR TRUTH

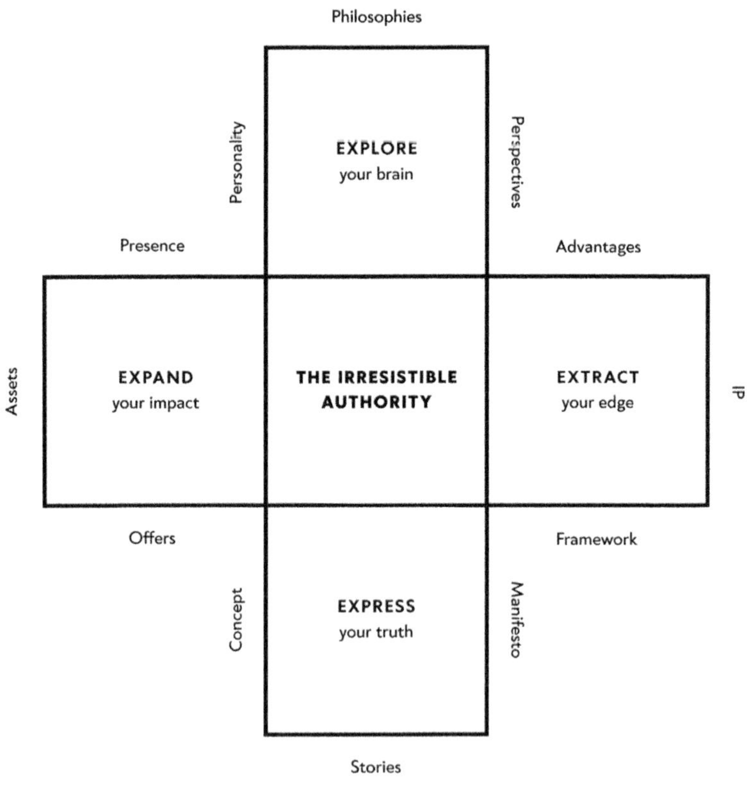

Manifesto: Clarify your thought leader mission and turn it into a manifesto that amplifies your distinct voice and activates your dream clients.

Stories: Articulate your wisdom with transparency, integrity, and conviction through content that deeply resonates with your audience.

Concept: Find a compelling angle that pulls your wisdom together in a way you can creatively infuse into your brand communications.

Core phase outcome: positioning concept.

You're not here to shout louder than your competitors; you're here to play an entirely different tune. No more diluting, censoring, or watering down what you're really here to say. Your intellect and creativity have the power to sucker-punch people in the soul. Don't let them wither because someone told you everything you write has to be understood by a five-year-old. Boring might get understood, but it rarely gets remembered.

11

MANIFESTO

You've likely heard a variation of this: I help [insert ideal client] achieve [desired result] by doing [your unique area of expertise]. While this is clear, it doesn't evoke emotion. This is a basic positioning statement, not a message. Creative differentiation is becoming ever-more important as the online blandscape, I mean landscape, expands, industries become even noisier, and attention spans reduce. Standing out and *staying* out is critical for sustainable success, which means that once you've extracted your edge, you've got to know how to communicate it in equally sharp ways and with consistent conviction.

Some marketers say to attract more of the right clients you just need to clarify your message, as if everything changes once this happens. And it's true that you need to have a clear message because confused people don't buy... *But neither do bored ones.* Think about it. If it takes up to 27 touchpoints for someone to build trust, do you really think they're going to hang around that long if your message doesn't stimulate an emotional response within them? Thought leadership isn't just about becoming an advocate for your ideas, it's about becoming an advocate for the identity your ideal clients desire. Your thoughts should provoke feelings. The dull *I help* statements can die now, please.

Clear isn't enough these days. Anyone can be clear about what they do and who they help. Clear doesn't stand out. Clear doesn't disrupt. Clear doesn't slow scrolls or hook hearts. If you want to captivate, be clear *and* clever. That's where personality and creativity come in. Think about the best ad campaigns you've seen. Remember when Dollar Shave Club came on the scene a few years ago? The reason their video went viral wasn't because they said *"We sell cheap subscription razors to blokes"* even though that's exactly what they do. It's because it was fun. Unexpected. Different. Laced with razor-sharp humour. Objections were dealt with head-on in an irreverent and random way. This was a brand that didn't take itself seriously, and the target market resonated with that. It was the complete opposite of competitor Gillette's approach, which was why it worked spectacularly. The website was so inundated with traffic it crashed in the first 48 hours. They got 12,000 new subscribers in the first few days. And the company ended up being sold for over a billion dollars. The campaign slogan was *Shave Time. Shave Money.* Clear. Clever.

Maybe you're thinking it's easy to be creative when selling a physical product. But what if you *are* the product? Creativity is a skill that so few personal brands leverage because they're too busy in the epidemic of generic, churning out content that's going to be lost and forgotten by the algorithm next week.

THE MECCA OF YOUR MESSAGE

Thought leaders don't need content templates or "I help" statements. They have power perspectives and manifestos born from their soul. Your brand manifesto is the Mecca of your message. The mission behind your thought leadership. Imagine it's the movie trailer for your brand, giving people a powerful taste of what to expect. The goal with this is to have anybody read / watch it and *know* whether they're meant to be in your world. Only a small selection of people should feel like they are, and you want this manifesto to stimulate them on a cellular level. You're not here to convince naysayers. You're here to make the right people feel seen, heard, understood, and *activated* in your presence. Whether that activates their brain or their behaviour doesn't matter, the point is that they're *moved* in some way. You have to move someone emotionally before you can move them physically. Your brand manifesto must:

- Be written with one person or problem in mind (consider the person you would most love to work with, or the most significant problem your expertise solves).
- Have clear flags of defiance and devotion.
- Reference your story – we need to know why you care so much.
- Include power perspectives you're passionate about.
- Have an activating frequency.

Just like your power perspectives and proprietary framework, your manifesto can be used as a positioning tool. It can feature on your website, or in a video, and you can use snippets wherever you have a presence. When you know what you think and how to articulate that in powerful ways, the way you can position yourself to become the must-have in your market is so much easier.

DEFIANT MOVERS EXAMPLE

Let me introduce you to Coach Kym, aka, The Defiant Coach. When we first started working together, Kym wanted to create a piece of the market she could dominate. She wanted to start shining as a thought-leading coach in a league of her own, rather than dancing in other people's shadows. Here's what we did together. First, we explored her brain. Kym is a force of nature, and she thinks, talks, acts, and coaches like it. She believes in taking bold, messy, sometimes terrifying action. She believes failure is essential for success. She believes in breaking rules, taking risks, and making massive moves. Her whole life has been about betting on herself, proving others wrong, and *commanding* her rightful seat at the table when she wasn't offered a chair.

From all of this exploration, we identified a golden thread of defiance through her life experiences. Business coaching is what she does, but defiance is who she is and how she thinks. That helped us extract her edge. Kym isn't some blah-blah business coach, so we didn't brand her like one. She's The Defiant Coach, and everything comes back to what that means. *"I am defiance. It's in my blood to challenge everything and everyone, so you better be ready because it's coming whether you like it or not. I believe defiance is differentiation. It's one of the reasons it's scary. Standing alone in power and integrity is better than standing amongst others in denial of their desires."*

We created and refined her concepts to align with this edge and created The Defiant Coach Approach: Your gateway to industry disruption, competitor domination, and more revenue, recognition, and respect than you can twerk your tail feather at.

We also gave her ideal clients an identity of Defiant Movers and wrote a vivid description of who they are at their core (a very helpful exercise for keeping your communications focused). Once the brand positioning was nailed, we moved on to expressing her truth. We started by creating a power-packed brand manifesto that led the messaging strategy. A person could read only this and know exactly what Kym stands for, what she stands against, and whether she's *the* person for them. (Kym listens to rap music while reading her manifesto every morning and if that isn't a vibe, I don't know what is.)

The tone of Kym's example is bold and strong, which is appropriate for her brand. Yours doesn't have to be the same! It's for you to play with possibility and create what feels right for you.

DEFIANT MOVERS DESCRIPTION

1. Defiant Movers know that taking a risk is as important as taking a breath. It's not optional if they want to run a business and live a life that thrills them.
2. Defiant Movers are always ready for battle. Even though they fight to win, they're unfazed if they lose because they're already proof that failure is 1) inevitable, and 2) rocket fuel for winning. They're willing to step into the arena of growth and feel the pain before they feel the pleasure. This alone makes them special.

3. Defiant Movers know that winning isn't something they do once. There is always more to learn, more to see, more to do. No matter what, they keep moving, falling, climbing. And once they're at the top of one mountain, they're itching to start at the bottom of another.
4. Defiant Movers always bet on themselves, and even though they can quit, they don't. They know that what they learn from losing their own game is infinitely more valuable than winning at someone else's. This is where their strength is born.
5. Defiant Movers have felt misunderstood their whole life. While others would want to follow a crowd, a Defiant Mover would want to follow their curiosity, which was never where the crowd was going. They show up where they're least expected to be and own it, no matter how exposed they feel.
6. Defiant Movers make decisions based on what's true for them, not what's true for a business guru. They also make those decisions based on a blend of intuition, instinct, and their own cold, hard data.
7. Defiant Movers do whatever it takes for however long it takes. They know that motivation is unreliable, and they take bold, consistent, against-the-grain action until they get the result they want or the lesson they need.
8. Defiant Movers are allergic to settling. Settling is for the masses; defiance is for the brave few who refuse to lie down in a box. The box might be comfortable, but if it's not custom-made, they'll light a match and watch it burn.
9. Defiant Movers resist openly and disobey boldly. They never stop moving, even in the face of fear,

doubt, and other people's unsolicited opinions. They dance cheek-to-cheek with things that terrify them. Daily. But ultimately, they know that all moves are good moves, even if they don't feel good when they make them.

10. Defiant Movers are the mavericks, leading the way for a new world. They champion the fight for freedom, love, creativity, equity, and opportunity. They believe with fervour that who you are and where you're from don't have to define who you will be and where you're capable of going.
11. Defiant Movers are potential in motion and legends in the making.

DEFIANT MOVERS MANIFESTO

Warning: read at your own risk.

Defiance. Noun. Open resistance. Bold disobedience.

When you've spent your whole life playing by someone else's rules, the way out isn't to break them...

It's to play a whole new game entirely. One where you don't just make the rules, you kick down all the doors, smash all the ceilings, *and* reap all the rewards because the game you've been playing has done everything possible to program you for conformity and mediocrity.

It's taught you to defy *yourself.*
To make you believe *you can't.*
To set you up to lose.
Over and over again:
Don't say that.

Don't do that.
You shouldn't be here.
That's not how we do things.
Sit down.
Stay in line.
Shhhhh.
Don't ruffle feathers.

Excuse me, if feathers aren't meant to be ruffled, what the fuck are they for?

It seems the rest of the world forgot that games are supposed to be thrilling and that players like you exist. Players with a taste for rolling the dice – because they know they can roll with the punches. A taste for upping the stakes – because they're willing to fall before they rise. A taste for staying in the ring – even when the odds are stacked against them.

It might feel dangerous the first time you play but danger is delicious when it shows you what you're made of. And you're made of grit, guts, and a fire that never goes out.

Someone tries to douse it with doubt? You blaze brighter.

Defiance isn't something you do. It's who you are. It's in your blood. It always has been, you just haven't let it dominate.

Until now.

Can you feel it? That heat on your skin. That drum in your chest. That voice in your head saying *it's time to take the risk.* Yeah, the risk everyone's told you not to take.

Brilliance is born out of bravery. Want to be effortlessly confident every day? You're going to have to get comfortable downing a cup of courage every morning first.

Sure, you can still have your coffee.

You don't need to be perfect; you don't need a plan; you definitely don't need permission.

But in order to win... You have to move.

Dauntlessly.
Decisively.
Defiantly.

Whether you want to change one mind or change the whole world, you better be ready because what you've always wanted is coming for you at lightning speed.

Cool?
Cool.
Your move.

ACTIONS

- Give your dream client an identity and write a vivid description of them.
- Write your brand manifesto as if you're going to perform it on stage in front of an audience full of those people (put on some epic movie music to help you get into a powerful energetic state!).

12

STORIES

"For sale: baby shoes, never worn." Who knew six words could stir up so much emotion? (This story is often attributed to Ernest Hemingway but is unlikely to have been written by him.) There's a reason why stories are such effective tools for communication. A story can make people feel whatever you want them to... if you tell it in the right way. A story, if it's powerful enough, can create an *imprint* on a human brain, which means you've not only been noticed, but you're also going to be remembered.

I'm not desperate to consume "content" every day, but stories? Those are different. A captivating story invites people into your world and makes them feel so at home they never want to leave. Stories are vehicles for your wisdom. You can have one core message and a million ways to communicate it. Stories are how you repeat yourself without ever saying exactly the same thing. Remember, you're intentionally becoming a person of interest here. You're not here to tell the whole story, you're here to tell an edited version. Being uncensored in your message doesn't mean sharing everything. That's where the pressure to perform comes from. Rather, it means that what you *do* choose to show should be genuine. When you bring more stories into your brand communications:

- You won't become bored of repeating your message over and over (which is important if you want to become known for it) because you can always find new ways to communicate it.
- Your audience will be continuously captivated by your brand because, although they will already know your message, they will be intrigued by the new stories you share it through.
- Stories bring meaning and emotional context to the message and allow nuances and layers and depth to be explored. Basically, they give it a heartbeat, especially important now that AI is in the picture.
- The right people will see themselves in your stories (when you tell the right ones) and this leads to trust and connection that runs deeper than any other kind of marketing tactic.

YOU ARE YOUR OWN MUSE

Everything that you need to captivate your people is already inside of you. If you've ever felt like you don't know how to come up with ideas or you struggle to get inspired, remind yourself of this every time that you come to create. You are the goldmine. You are your own muse. You don't need to regurgitate content that already exists on the internet. You don't need to compare yourself to others in your industry. You don't need to wonder whether you have anything interesting to say, and you definitely don't need to look to anybody else for the answers. You are literally surrounded by stories. There's a story in everything if you're willing to look close enough. You don't have to be funny, divisive, or really "out there" for the right people to want to hear what you have to say. They want your truth, not smoke and mirrors. But truth doesn't mean sharing everything. Be ruthless in your editing.

Even if you don't see yourself as a leader, your people do. Your people look to you as a leader that they can walk beside. What you share needs to reflect that reality. You need to lead yourself *first*. That means sharing from a place of strength and wisdom, even when you don't feel strong or wise. This will make your presence so much more powerful. If you choose to share hard times and struggles, and it's important to sometimes, do so through a learning lens, not a hot mess one. Your people don't expect perfection, but they are in your world to grow. You already know who your people are, and you already know what the key message is that you're here to share with them, but that message can be shared in so many different ways. Don't worry about boring people by repeating yourself. You don't become known for something by talking about it once. Embracing that makes articulating your wisdom so much more expansive and exciting. Your stories are not only unique, but they are also limitless, so you don't have to put yourself in a box with strict formulas, rigid templates, or fill-in-the-blank captions. Stories stir change. And when you know how to connect your stories to what you sell, a whole new world will open up to you.

THE STORYMARKETING MATRIX

Ditch the content pillars. They're just another box to limit your thinking. (If they work for you, great! But if they feel restrictive, listen to that.) If you're grounded in your wisdom, all you need is to ask yourself high-quality questions. What's special about your expertise? Why did you grow your knowledge and skills in this particular area? What's the thread that connects your past, present, and future?

Let's say you're a resilience coach. This is fairly niche in itself. You're unlikely to be a resilience coach if you've never faced adversity. What did you experience? How did that impact you? How did you handle it? What does resilience mean to you? Can it really be learned? How has it shaped your decisions? Why is resilience the key to a better life? What does resilience look like when you're scared? Has there been a time when you let your fear win? What's the difference between resilience and courage? I could go on and on. Asking these questions will open up a world of stories that only you can tell, and that will be both relevant and resonant to your people. This is how your brand narrative can really take shape.

If having some structure helps, I developed the Storymarketing Matrix which has four quadrants: elevated expert positioning, seductive personal stories, unapologetic opinions, and irresistible offers.

You might feel like you default to educational content because it's easy to provide tips and tricks, and while that's showing your expertise to an extent, it's not elevating your authority positioning. You might feel like you put out a lot of inspirational content which gets good engagement, but not enough people are actually buying. You might have strong opinions, but there's some fear around sharing them beyond conversations with peers. You might find that while you have something awesome to sell, you don't sell it with unwavering belief. Covering all four quadrants will help you balance the content you put out there so you're able to fully express yourself, connect on a deeper level with the right people, and move them closer to the sale with everything you write.

Each quadrant has its own objective, energy, and springboard.

Quadrant 1: Elevated Expert Positioning

What you know and what you do (and how it's different). This is more about being an authority figure with a unique blend of knowledge and skills than a generic educator.

Objective: Build trust and credibility. There's an abundance of information online, but people want transformation, not information. Remember who you're talking to. Buyers are getting more sophisticated and they're not looking for a tip on how to do something themselves. They're looking to understand why you're the perfect person for them to work with.

Energy: Authority energy. *"I am the authority. I'm grounded in my expertise and the value of it."*

Springboard questions: What does my best-fit client need to know today? What story can I tell that will position me as an expert in their eyes?

Quadrant 2: Seductive Personal Stories

Who you are. This is about going beneath the surface and showing the person behind the business. You can be vulnerable without baring it all.

Objective: Emotionally resonate. You want people to be moved by your words, but that doesn't mean everything has to be super deep and meaningful. There are lots of stories you can tell that entertain and activate. People don't need to have had the exact same experiences to feel seen, heard, and understood.

Energy: Human energy. *"I'm a human before I'm a business owner."*

Springboard questions: What does my best-fit client need to feel seen and understood today? What story can I tell that will help them see a version of themselves in it?

Quadrant 3: Unapologetic Opinions

How you think. This is about showing how your brain works (the premise of this whole book). Your opinions aren't facts, but they are your truths.

Objective: Shift or affirm beliefs. You want to share your power perspectives in an unapologetic way. Showcase what you stand for and against in ways that help people see what's possible and overcome what's currently in the way of the result they desire. You're drawing the right people closer with every uncensored communication. You don't have to be forceful. Your lived experience is valid and that's how your opinions are formed. Unapologetic opinions help you explain why you think a certain way, without suggesting you have all the answers. You're empathising and being a guide to the right people. Once you start saying the things you really want to say and realise that you don't die as a result, expressing yourself and showing up in your marketing becomes so much more fun.

Energy: Leader energy. *"When my people see me operating from a place of self-leadership, it helps them do the same."*

Springboard questions: What does my best-fit client need to experience a perspective shift or affirmation today? What story can I tell that will show what I stand for or against?

Quadrant 4: Irresistible Offers

What you do. How you actually work with people to get them a result. People aren't buying a service or a product from you, they're buying a different version of themselves. You want to make that version feel irresistible. You want them to see themselves differently after your story.

Objective: Sell. Or if you prefer to think of it this way, serve up a delightful invitation. People are allowed to turn down an invitation, but that wouldn't make you not want to throw a party. You have something a select few people want. Focus on serving the invitations to those people in a way that makes the experience sound unmissable.

Energy: Transformer energy. *"I have the ability to create change for a select group of people and it's my job to show them why this, why me, why now, and what's possible for them beyond working together."*

Springboard questions: What does my best-fit client need to solve their problem or fulfil their desire today? What story can I tell that will make it clear I can provide the result they want?

If you want to master the art of Storymarketing to stimulate higher demand and desire for your work, I have a course which will help you do exactly that. You can access it here:

www.captivationhouse.com/storymarketing-goldmine

CABINET OF CURIOSITIES

Stories are everywhere, the question is, are you looking and listening? What do you like to consume, inside or outside your industry? Why? What thoughts and feelings does it provoke? Have you ever asked yourself that? Analyse your own behaviour as a starting point. When you consciously start to look and listen, so many more stories will show up for you. If you ever run out of ideas for what to write, create, or share next and then find yourself venturing outside your own life-and-business bubble and hunting like a truffle pig for 1) inspiration and 2) validation for your existence, then it's time to open up your cabinet of curiosities. In sixteenth and seventeenth-century Europe, many of the wealthy and educated had what was called a Wunderkammern, which translates to a "wonder chamber" or "cabinet of curiosities". This served as a place to display the trinkets and treasures they'd collected from around the world – jewels, art, books, artefacts, that kind of thing. The cabinet of curiosities was their way of saying to others: *This is what intrigues and delights me, does it intrigue and delight you, too?* Unless you're a pensioner, you probably don't have an actual cabinet of curiosities in your home (although it will be peppered with items you could put in one), but it doesn't matter, because you certainly have one in your brain. I'm talking about:

- The places you've been.
- The sights you've seen.
- The people you've met.
- The experiences you've had.
- The food you've tasted.
- The music you've heard.
- The quotes you've memorised.
- The influences you've let shape you.
- The decisions you've made.
- The fears you've battled.
- The challenges you've overcome.
- The mistakes you've learnt from.
- The successes you've created.
- And the stories you can tell based on all of those.

Every day, you're adding to your cabinet of curiosities, but instead of physical objects, they're mental golden nuggets you're collecting from your journey. You *can* go searching for inspiration in unusual places, or you can dig something out of your cabinet of curiosities and tell an intriguing and delightful story about it. When you do, you won't just be telling a story, you'll be sharing a tiny piece of your soul. In an online world where it often feels like marketing is a transaction rather than an experience, a tiny piece of your soul could be exactly what people want, need, and are willing to pay money for.

WHAT'S THE POINT?

The way you share your perspectives through your stories will drive the narrative that creates your perceived value. There's no limit to what you can talk about so long as there's a point – something that threads the beginning to the end. You could start with a story you want to tell and find a lesson that fits. Or you could start with the lesson you want to share and find a story to illustrate it. For example, a story could be about me, about to get married knowing that there was a flood warning in place for my wedding day, which had been postponed twice already. This (true!) story has absolutely nothing to do with my business. But the thread that I could find within is staying strong, holding the vision for something, even when it feels hard, and surrendering control. That's definitely something my clients can relate to.

Say I wanted to share a perspective about making incremental upgrades in my life. I could shape a story about the time I decided in the supermarket that I was going to buy the luxury soap instead of the default cheap one, and how I never went back because I saw myself differently after that decision. There's always going to be some kind of thread that you can find to link a story to a lesson.

A few years ago, I did an at-home photo shoot. I changed my outfit so many times it made me sweat, and I took 314 photos of myself in two hours. There was a point when I wondered if any of the 314 would be usable. Plenty were not, but to my surprise, a bunch of them were. The big difference? *The angle.* Obviously, light and facial expression matter, but it became clearer the more photos I took that the angle was crucial. It's just the same with stories. Topic matters, and word choice matters, but the good ones – the captivating ones – always have a strong angle. It's the lens through which the story is told. The theme that gives the story meaning. The more unique, the more interesting. Don't attempt to write a story without knowing why you're writing it, who you're writing it for, what the point is, and which angle you think will work best.

TINY TRANSFORMATIONS

Every single one of your stories creates a tiny transformation. You've probably heard of marginal gains and the compound effect. The tiniest of changes aren't noticeable day-to-day, but when looked at over a long period of time, they make a significant difference. If you get 1% better each day for one year, you'll end up 37 times better by the time you're done. Not so tiny! Let's apply that thinking to your self-expression. Potency is more important than consistency, but one piece of content does not have to create a ground-breaking transformation within someone. That's possible, but if that's what you're shooting for, you're putting too much pressure on yourself. It's too heavy an expectation, and it might be why you're not showing up in the way you want to.

When you see your stories as an evolving *body of work*, with every touchpoint causing its own tiny transformation in the brain and body then, over time, that transformation grows. This is what it means to lead someone to a sale. You're sharing different things in different ways to instil trust in you, them, and your work, and it's the compound effect of the tiny transformations that matters.

Sharing content in the hope you'll see immediate results is probably why you won't see results, or not on the timeline you think they "should" happen in. Results rarely happen overnight. Sometimes a person can enter your world and buy from you within days, maybe even less. For others, it takes years. That's okay. Don't try to control their timeline. You can't. Your job is to continue to show up, share your truth, and trust that the right people are reading, watching, and changing. Treat everyone in your audience like a client. Some are paying with their money. Some are paying with their attention.

THE POWER OF ANALOGIES

Another evening, another refusal. Those big brown eyes bore into my soul, but the mouth stayed shut. It was becoming a frustrating pattern, and I needed a solution. When my son was weaning onto solid foods, it was common for me to spend up to an hour pottering around the kitchen making a **fingers crossed** delicious meal that all the family could eat – something with variety, nutrition, and that was quick. I went through a phase of making mince-based dishes – beef, pork, lamb, you name it, but when I served these up to my son, he wasn't interested. As a first-time mum, this sent me into a mild panic. He needed to eat! I would never force him to eat, but how could I make him eat? Then I had an idea. The slow cooker. Rather than cooking the meat under pressure on the stove for 20 minutes, why not try putting it in the slow cooker for eight hours? The additional time and care would make the meat softer and more tender and give it a greater depth of flavour. I tried it and voila. Bowls were scraped clean.

This became an analogy for one of my group experiences, The Sanctuary. You could go into the pressure cooker of some kind of "business accelerator" where the focus is on speed, productivity, and generating results through intensity, or you could come into the slow cooker of The Sanctuary, where the focus was on taking your time, the depth of the experience, and creating results in a way that respects your personality and capacity.

Analogies are an incredible tool for communicating what you do and how you think in a way people can understand on a human level. They don't need to have your expertise to understand your point. When you show how you think by relating what you do (unfamiliar) to something people instantly understand (familiar) through stories and analogies, it helps instil this feeling of safety. The Cambridge Dictionary defines an analogy as: *"A comparison between things that have similar features, often used to help explain a principle or idea."* Analogies are particularly powerful when trying to communicate:

- A complex idea in a simple, easy-to-grasp way.
- A relatively unknown idea in a globally recognised way.
- An intangible or more abstract concept in a tangible or concrete way.
- Something common or conventional in a more creative way.

One of my previous clients, Lara Rickard, helps women heal their PCOS using the wisdom of their body *before* any diet or lifestyle changes. Her prospective clients were so used to the narrative that healing comes from diet and lifestyle changes that she faced a real challenge explaining why developing deep trust with their bodies was the missing piece in their healing journey. Here's what was happening for her:

- Potential client does a Google search around their particular health issue and Lara's website comes up.
- They click on the website and book a discovery call.
- On the call, they have a bunch of questions and objections around her approach and how it actually works (even though it's explained on the site).
- Lara feels she has to "convince" that her approach is valuable (and worth the premium price tag), even if it's unfamiliar.
- Client decides to try something else first and only come back to Lara as a "last resort".

Basically, her potential clients were extremely problem-aware and had tried a lot of "solutions" already, but they weren't necessarily aware that Lara's solution even existed as an option to consider before now. This is common if you're pioneering an approach in your space, which means that even if other solutions haven't worked, it still feels scary for someone to invest a premium in something so different from what they've already tried. So, Lara's positioning needed to shift, and her messaging needed to be upgraded to educate those who were problem-aware about Lara's solution and build their belief in it as a trustworthy option. One of the ways we chose to approach this was to create a beautiful, layered visual metaphor for her approach, rooted in her heritage and brand story. This meant she could apply something familiar and easy to understand to an approach that was new and more difficult to grasp. Here's an extract example. (She used a Marula tree because it's native to Zimbabwe where she grew up.)

"Imagine your Body as a Marula tree where the soil surrounding the tree represents your relationship with your body. Just as quality soil provides stability, nourishment, and a strong foundation for the tree to grow, take root, and flourish in its own unique way, cultivating a nurturing body relationship serves as the same fertile starting point on your PCOS journey. Of course, nutrient-rich soil isn't the sole requirement for the tree's thriving. The Marula tree needs additional essential elements like sunlight and water to fuel its growth. In the context of PCOS, these elements can be likened to the indicated food and lifestyle changes. And there are other factors to consider such as pollinators, wind, and even mycelium, representing emotional, energetic, and spiritual factors. Implementing food and lifestyle changes without cultivating body connection and trust is like giving a tree water and sunshine without first ensuring it is grounded in nourishing soil. Without that strong foundation, the tree won't be able to fully absorb, utilise, and benefit from these elements. So, just as quality soil promotes the vibrancy and resilience of a Marula tree, starting with a solid body relationship as your foundation empowers you to make sustainable, loving, and meaningful changes to reversing PCOS symptoms."

Once she incorporated this analogy, Lara experienced an immediate shift in how prospective clients were able to understand the depth of her work, how it was different from other approaches, and the value she offered. She also created a gorgeous graphic to further translate her perspective and bring a visual aspect to the analogy, which is especially important for those who process information visually or struggle to create images in their own mind. This is where infographics hold power, and they're vastly underused with personal brands. Turning your thoughts into visuals helps you get to the crux of an idea. If you had to turn your idea into an image, how would you do it?

ACTIONS

- Choose a few stories you're excited to tell, ideally one from each quadrant.
- Choose an analogy that helps illustrate the more abstract side of your expertise.

13

CONCEPT

"T*hank you for the peppercorns!*" Cue my confusion. I'd met a fellow business owner a few times at some local networking events, but I had definitely not sent him peppercorns in the post. Why was he emailing me assuming I had? Simple. My company was called PepperJar. *Spicing words so they're irresistible to read and impossible to ignore.* (I've since rebranded to Captivation House.) He had such a strong mental association between me and pepper that he assumed I sent him peppercorns in the post. This is why a lot of my work revolves around finding a strong positioning concept. It gives people a reason to think of you. And the closer you are to the top of their mind, the easier it is for them to talk about you and buy from you.

Do you *need* a creative positioning concept? No. You can still position yourself in desirable ways through content, stories, and visuals, and you may feel more comfortable with that as a personal brand, but a concept can do so much heavy lifting for you, especially if what you do is in a more competitive industry. Take Kym for example. If we had positioned her as "just another" business coach, she would have to work a lot harder to stand out. Instead, she's the Defiant Coach. The concept of defiance is creatively infused *everywhere* and that's how she's able to have strangers land on her website and pay her thousands after a short conversation. Because of her positioning, the right people instantly know she's the one they want to work with. She's The One, not one of many.

The more reasons you give someone to notice and remember you, the better. It's the big idea you can become known for, the umbrella that everything else – perspectives, ideas, stories – can fall underneath. It's there to give direction to your communications, bring cohesion to your presence, and expand alongside you. If necessary, you can change it in the future, just like I did with Captivation House. I am the face of the brand, I am the thought leader, but the concept stands on its own. This also allows for some separation from your brand. The brand is not you, it's an extension, a *reflection* of you, expressed in a creative way. A positioning concept can also become the signature, the fingerprint, *the thing* that your brand is recognised for. Having a concept helps create that important mental association, and it's how you put yourself in a memorable category of one without restricting yourself to talking about one thing. You can infuse elements of your personality through language, visuals, and the whole experience of your brand. This is who you are and how you think brought to life in a distinctive way.

THE CREATIVE DIRECTION

There are infinite ways to approach a positioning concept. We need to remember that the point is not just to escape the epidemic of generic, it's to shape perception in a certain way. The concept has to support the way you want to be seen by your ideal clients. It would have made no sense for Kym's concept to revolve around defiance if she didn't want to work with bold go-getters. It would have made no sense for her messaging to be soft and cutesy. It would have made no sense for her visual brand to contain pastel colours or photos of a smiley Kym on her laptop in a cafe. Remember you're intentionally making yourself a person of interest. What unique spin would set you apart from your competitors, excite you to embody, and draw the right people closer? Here are some questions to ask yourself to start cranking your creative cogs:

- What do people already associate me with? Do I like that? How could I amplify it?
- What different ways could I express my golden thread?
- What is my most interesting competitive advantage? Is there a creative way to translate that?
- If there was one power perspective I could be known for, what would it be? How could I build a concept around that?
- What do I see all the time in my industry? What's something wildly different from that?
- What are the most interesting or fascinating visual interpretations of who I am and the way I think?

I'm going to explore five ways you can approach developing a positioning concept: identity, movement, theme, idea, and style – but these are not exhaustive. I want you to play and have fun with this part! They can also overlap. For example, someone could have a distinct identity and use a theme. Or they could lead a strong movement as well as have a distinct style. There are no rules.

IDENTITY

This is a popular approach for personal brands because it's centred around a singular identity that isn't their own name. This allows for both personality infusion and separation. You can dial up the character traits you want to show more of and dial down those you want to keep to yourself. This is as close to "being your own niche" as you get. When you're grounded in your wisdom and create an identity around your sweet spot of expertise, you won't feel the need to switch it up every few months. It's an opportunity to be playful in the way you market yourself. You create an audience of people whom the identity speaks to and you become uncopyable because the brand is truly about your identity, which is not possible to replicate authentically. This identity can also hint at the experience to expect in your world. Let's look at some examples.

Gulce Onganer, The Video Architect

Gulce trained to be an architect before shifting into entrepreneurship and takes a very structured approach to her work. She's to the point, strong in her opinions, and can take you through every single step of building a leading YouTube channel.

Dajé Alōh, The Story Doula

Dajé describes herself as a "visionary midwife" and she is focused on emboldening leaders to birth their visions into the world. Her work is rooted in the ancient wisdom of the earth, her word choices are beautifully distinct, and there is a softness to her strength.

Ashley Beaudin, The Gentle Business Coach

We met Ashley earlier in this book. Her whole being exudes gentleness. Even her power perspectives are delivered with compassion. She wants people to know she's a soft place to land in a world of pressure and stress.

Erika Lyremark, The Daily Whip

Erika used to be a stripper and instead of hiding that, she shaped her whole brand around it. She's bossy, knows how to get what she wants (and how to get the best out of those she works with), and takes an editorial approach to her presence. Her book is called *Think Like A Stripper*, she tells fascinating stories from her time stripping which she relates to business, and her offers have names like TripleXpert.

Erin McCarthy, PhD, The CALM Coach

Calm is Erin's golden thread. She used to be a philosophy professor and her work revolves around helping people become the calmest version of themselves. She's not "just" a mindfulness and somatic coach, she's the best at bringing calm to your chaos. Taking on the identity of The CALM

Coach is her stake in the ground, and she can turn CALM into a proprietary framework.

Jade Tambini, B2B Jade

Jade has decades of experience in B2B marketing and when she became so popular on TikTok for the identity of B2B Jade, she built her whole personal brand around it.

A note on the power of having an identity concept. I randomly came across a podcast interview ad from Steven Bartlett. The episode was titled: *The Coffee Expert: The Surprising Link Between Coffee, Mental Health, Depression, and Heart Disease*. I loved the strong yet simple positioning, so I clicked through to the interviewee's profile. It was just his name, James Hoffman. The Coffee Expert was a memorable identity Steven had given him for the purposes of the podcast promotion. Maybe this is an identity that's given to James in other places too, but I'm so much more likely to remember The Coffee Expert than I am James Hoffman. The concept positions him in my mind in a way his name can't.

Questions to ask yourself to create an identity concept:

- If people remembered me for one simple thing, what would it be?
- What identity could I assume that distinguished me from others offering similar services in my industry?
- What piece of my past do I feel so connected to that it has to form a part of my public persona?

MOVEMENT

A movement concept centres around the change you want to see in your industry or your client's world. It's a way of positioning your brand as bigger than you and putting a spotlight on your mission. While it's born from your wisdom, it's carried by others. It may speak to the movement itself, or the result you're fighting for or against. This is a great way of grounding your brand in what matters most so you can rally the right people around you and repel the rest. You know how I spoke about polarisation with your perspectives? It is the same thing with your positioning concept. It creates a feeling of belonging, like you're a part of something special – perfect if having a big impact is one of your core drivers and you want your brand to be known for more than what it does. It can build an army of brand ambassadors who essentially do your marketing for you because they talk to their friends and peers about you and make them want to get on board the movement. Here are some examples.

Ash Ambirge, The Middle Finger Project

Ash is a whole vibe. She's actually the reason I got into online business. She's a teacher and writer, and witty irreverence runs through the blood of her brand. Everything she communicates is through the lens of unapologetically giving the finger to settling for what society told you to be satisfied with and having the guts to go after what you want. She has a book of the same name and a diehard community who identify with (or aspire to) unconventional living. As soon as you hear The Middle Finger Project, you know what to expect. It'll either turn you on or turn you off, and that's the whole point. The people who dig it will become obsessed. She uses language like *"live the unfuckwithable life you deserve"* and *"follow your passion unless you're a serial killer"*.

Jo Bendle, Meant For More®

Jo also has an identity she now uses (The Business Energiser®) but she'd built a beautiful movement long before that. Meant For More® speaks to ambitious, driven, business owners who know that more is out there for them, no matter what stage of life they're at. Many business coaches speak to this group, but Jo infuses the phrase "meant for more" every-where, truly embodies the movement, and owns the trademark.

Lacey Sites, A Lit Up Life

Lacey's business name speaks to the outcome her clients want (they don't just want a thriving business; they want it to light up their lives). She also has a podcast called LITerally which is a playful development of the concept. Her 1:1 waitlist has *hundreds* of people on it, so she's positioned herself excellently!

The three people in the above examples are all within the business coaching space. They don't have flashy visual brands, but they each have distinct positioning concepts that speak to who they are and the way they think.

Jessie Inchauspé, Glucose Goddess®

Jessie's a French biochemist whose area of expertise is glucose, but she pairs this with the word goddess to give an unusual twist on the expectation of a biochemist. She has a book of the same name, and her goal is to make cutting-edge science accessible. This is a great example of a crossover between identity and movement.

Natalie Bullen, Unapologetic Wealth®

Natalie is a sales expert whose work focuses on selling premium services and building wealth. She stands for those who know wealth is their birthright (she even has a private podcast called Birthright). Natalie has a strong voice, she's steadfast in her opinions, and she makes it consistently clear what change she's here to make and why.

Rachael Shepard-Ohta, Hey Sleepy Baby

Rachael is on a mission to normalise normal baby sleep and takes a stand against traditional sleep training methods. She's open about how sleep training her first baby inspired her journey, which is a great example of turning an origin story into a competitive advantage. She's the keeping-it-real safe place for parents who don't want to sleep train but need alternatives for their own sanity.

Joeli Brearley, Pregnant Then Screwed®

Still one of the best names I've ever come across. This is a charitable organisation which Joeli is the founder and face of.

You immediately know from the name that this is a movement for people who have been let down by the system because they got pregnant. The concept clearly expresses the fight that this charity is taking on (flag of defiance) and is a voice for the collective.

Questions to ask yourself to create a movement concept:

- What is the change I want to see in the world that I can't help but talk about?
- What does my ideal client aspire to be or have that I know I can support them with?
- What is a movement I know I can lead but that's far bigger than me?

THEME

A theme concept allows you to easily create something that stands out in your market. It's something the brain can latch on to and remember easily. It makes developing your brand language easier and more fun, and you can be specific and playful with the way you make your brand cohesive by using this theme through all the touchpoints. The theme concept can be a brilliant choice for businesses that really value individuality and creativity, particularly in more saturated industries where it feels like everyone is stuck in the epidemic of generic. It's also great for businesses that offer intangible results because a theme can help people visualise what you do.

Suzi Gray, Captivation House (me!)

I help people build captivating brands and articulate the value of what they do in creative ways. Branding is pretty abstract, so I wanted a concept that brought some tangibility to my work (branding is like building a house, from laying the foundations to designing the interiors). I've used language like:

> *Unlock your inner goldmine.*
> *Knock down your virtual door.*
> *Build a brand that feels like home.*
> *Behind closed doors.*
> *Take a seat at my table.*

The visual style includes plants, doors, keys, and photos of me in my home for a cosy and approachable vibe. I paired core phrases with particular images to dial up the distinctiveness. I also wanted to bring delight into the overall experience, so I have a treasure hunt on my website which means people have to find various clues before using a code to unlock the "trapdoor". Branding is never done, and I know it will be time for me to evolve Captivation House into its more grown-up version soon. The concept will remain, but the expression will evolve.

Gemma Went, The Lighthouse Business Academy®

Gemma and I worked together because she wanted to create a brand separate from her personal brand that would still be an extension of her philosophies and perspectives. She wanted to create an industry-leading business consultant certification that focused on effective ethical approaches. Gemma already had an excellent reputation in her personal brand, and we wanted to transfer that into this one. I developed the lighthouse positioning concept as a metaphor for *"shining the light"* on a new way of doing business and being a *"beacon of trust"* for her people. It's been incredibly successful, and Gemma has consistently sold out her certification spaces.

Jen Olmstead and Jeff Shipley, TONIC

TONIC sells stunning Showit website and social media templates. As you might assume from the name, they use a drinks theme in their business. Some of their templates are named after cocktails, like Amaretto Sour, and they have a drink-themed quiz to help you discover your perfect match template. This light-hearted concept is perfect for this brand which clearly loves to have fun. They have perspectives like: *"Life is too short to hate your website."*

Questions to ask yourself to create a theme concept:

- Is there a passion or interesting part of me that I would love to centre my brand around?
- Is there a fun, unusual, or even obvious way of expressing what I do that has nothing to do with what I actually do?
- Is there a metaphor or analogy that makes sense in the context of my brand that could become a leading theme for it?

IDEA

Your brain is your biggest brand asset. The more you lean in and leverage your IP, the more valuable it can become and the easier it is to become known for the way you think. It can help you stand out from others who do similar work in similar ways. When your ideas are different, branding them helps position you as the irresistible authority. This could be a concept, approach, framework, methodology, or modality. The idea concept is a smart choice for business owners who have pioneered a way of thinking and delivering and want to lead the market with it. It's something that can be branded on its own and become an entity that doesn't necessarily require you to be the face of it. You could train/certify people in your idea, license an approach, and even set the foundations to sell, if that's something you want to do.

What is your biggest idea? What concept do you always find yourself talking about? What's your leading power perspective? What is the thing that could become a book or keynote speech? The angle you want to be known for and could build your entire brand around? Making this choice doesn't mean it's the *only* thing you want to become known for, but the decision to hone in on your unique brilliance will help you easily escape the epidemic of generic and give you a clear edge. The key to turning an idea into a positioning concept is to keep it super simple. We want to get to the most distilled version.

Simon Sinek, Start With Why

"People don't buy what you do, they buy why you do it." You've probably seen his TED talk. This power perspective, which

was an unconventional way of looking at buyer behaviour, put Simon Sinek on the map and it later became his first book. The way he thinks about why people buy became what he was known for, and his approach has become standard practice in many organisations considering their own market position. It's a great example of how powerful simplicity can be when expressed with conviction.

Sally Hogshead, How to Fascinate®

Remember Sally? She pioneered the How to Fascinate® test, a personal branding test to help you see what's different about you and use it to impress and influence people. Her whole brand is positioned around her idea of fascination advantages, and associated words like impress, hidden talents, and primary and secondary advantages are used often. Sally had huge success in the advertising industry when she was younger and has used this expertise to create a system that is all about getting attention from the right people.

Natasha Leigh Bray, HeartHealing®

Natasha is the creator of HeartHealing®, an innovative integrative healing approach to achieving wholeness. It combines scientific, spiritual, and energetic principles which result in deeper and faster shifts than mind-based techniques are able to offer. Focusing on the heart is unconventional in the healing industry, which makes it easy for Natasha to be a thought leader in this area. Although Natasha is the face of the brand, she may choose not to be in the future as the positioning concept stands on its own.

Mai-kee Tsang, Sustainable Visibility®

Mai-kee is a podcast guesting strategist and ICF certified trauma-conscious leadership coach for visionaries who want to create a deeper difference by leading through a more diverse, inclusive, and equitable lens. Sustainable Visibility® is the way her people create that and is something they know they *want*. This is a term Mai-kee's trademarked and forms the core of her brand communications.

Questions to ask yourself to create an idea concept:

- If there was only one idea I became known for, what would I want it to be?
- What is pioneering about the way I think and create change in the world?
- What is the simplest way to communicate what my work exists to do in the world?

STYLE

A style positioning concept is perfect if the way you think about your work is obvious in the distinctive way you perform it. A style concept is easy to recognise, like how you hear a song you've never heard before but know who's singing it because you recognise their sound. It's got a special vibe that can make it appear more exclusive (and you can charge higher prices for that). A style concept is often appealing to those in creative industries, like designers, stylists, photographers, and writers, though it could be extremely effective for those outside it, too. You can lean into your natural strengths and leverage them. Some people communicate more strongly through how something looks versus how something reads. This is still wisdom. But if your focus is thought leadership, this concept is best paired with another. There's only so much "speaking for itself" a style can do before it needs additional substance.

Damaly Shepherd

When I see a Damaly headshot, I know it's a Damaly headshot. If I lived closer to NYC, I'd have booked her! She has a talent for bringing out the most powerful and radiant parts of the people she photographs and makes it obvious that she believes iconic headshots are an essential part of stepping into the next version of yourself. When you have the style distinguished, the key is pairing it with words that will do the style justice. Damaly uses messaging like: *"It's time to have images that reflect not just where and who you are, but who you are becoming and where you are going. Through the lens of Damaly's camera, you will truly be seen in all the amazing ways the rest of the world already sees you."*

Shauna Haider, We Are Branch

Shauna is a designer who has a very intricate, high-end design style and people hire her because they want that kind of sophisticated elegance for their own brand. It's obvious she pours so much effort into her work. Shauna strengthened her style with the theme of We Are Branch, The Branch Method, and the tagline: *"Grow your brand to new heights."*

Leonie Dawson

Leonie brings a whole new meaning to colourful! She's a marketing teacher who has created a world of her own through the way she communicates, both verbally and visually. She clearly places a high value on self-expression and has a specific style of doing it. This gives people a sense of who she is without knowing anything about her. If they like what they see, they'll stick around. Even though she'll be one of thousands of marketing teachers, her style truly sets her apart.

The J. Peterman Company

This isn't a personal brand but is an exquisite example of the style positioning concept. Rather than using photographs and descriptions for their clothes, like every other clothing brand, they create stunningly detailed drawings of their products and pair them with whimsical, escapist stories like this one. *"Cheers to Fate. You won't need to climb the railing on the aft deck of an ocean liner in this (in fact, I discourage it outright) or require rescue by a young, handsome artist who has a way with the words. No, consider instead the life this dress is truly meant to inhabit. Waltzes. Witty repartee. Winsome, knowing looks over the rim of a crystal coupe. Everything grand, elegant. Romantic, mysterious. Whether you pose for the artist later, well, that's entirely up to you. Rose Met Jack Dress (No. J7477)."*

Questions to ask yourself to create a style concept:

- What is already distinct about the way I naturally show up?
- Is there an important part of myself I'm not expressing that I really want to?
- How would I show people the way I think if I couldn't say a word?

BEYOND THE CONCEPT

A positioning concept is a strong cornerstone for your brand, but the real impact is made when you support it with:

- Captivating messaging, including keywords and phrases that translate this concept in concise and memorable ways.
- Offers that are a match for the way you want to position yourself (e.g., if Natalie spoke about unapologetic wealth but had low-cost offers that promised the world, it wouldn't make sense).
- Authority assets that are an extension of your positioning concept.
- Your energy (e.g., if you have a bold concept, you need to embody boldness in the way you show up).
- Visuals that communicate the concept in an elevated way (this includes visual brand identity, graphics, and photos).
- A talisman that can become its own association with your brand (e.g., author Seth Godin's colourful glasses).
- Brand experience that meets the expectation created by everything else and adds delight.

One of the best ways to communicate your wisdom alongside your positioning concept is through language. Your brand language is a collection of words and phrases that become unique to you and your business. Your brand language will include:

- Power perspectives (key messages you repeat).
- Words and phrases you habitually find yourself using (e.g., Ash Ambirge from The Middle Finger Project often writes "thank vodka" which suits her irreverent presence).
- Words and phrases you find yourself repeating in your line of work.
- Words and phrases you could use to infuse that unique twist of your positioning concept through your communications.

Pay particular attention to words and phrases your clients or audience reflect back to you. If they start using the same kind of language in the context of you or your work, that's a great sign. Stick with it. You can also create a never list. Words and phrases you would never use in your communications and that you would not want to be associated with you.

Next, consider the tone and wattage you want to use through your written communications. This, as always, comes back to the perception you're shaping with your brand. Tone is the way you communicate something rather than the words themselves. Before you write anything, decide what tone you want to use based on how you're trying to make someone feel. Excited? Hopeful? Certain? Wattage is the energetic frequency of the words themselves. For example, I could say: *"She walked into the room and sat on the sofa."* You understand me, but it doesn't make you feel anything. If you increase the wattage of just two of those words, you can maximise the impact of the sentence. So instead, I could say: *"She shuffled into the room and collapsed on the sofa."* See how the whole energy of that sentence shifts? You suddenly get a better sense of the character and their exhaustion, just by increasing the wattage of the words.

My favourite resources for helping you shape your language bank are:

- The classic online thesaurus for simple word substitutions.
- *The Emotion Thesaurus* by Angela Ackerman and Becca Puglisi for when you're trying to express a feeling. This book gives you examples of what actually happens when someone feels a certain emotion. If you struggle to show rather than tell, this will be helpful.
- The online idioms dictionary for interesting ways to express your brand. For example, if I type in "house" I get different ideas for how I could infuse this concept into my communications. Housewarming party is one suggestion, so, when I launched my new brand and sent an email to my list, rather than making a standard announcement, I sent a housewarming invitation.
- Rhymezone to find words you could pair. Techniques like rhythm and alliteration make such a difference in the way the brain remembers things.

You want your words to have an emotional impact, whether you're actively selling something or not. You don't want to be a part of the epidemic of generic, so when it comes to your communications, try not to fall into the trap of using the same words as others because you think that's the way it has to be said.

With Kym, when we moved to the larger communication strategy and her first authority asset (website), we knew the language needed to pack a punch. Here are some snippets of how we infused both her strong personality and the golden thread of defiance into the website copy while making sure we were speaking directly to the exact kind of person Kym wanted to partner with most.

"You radiate audacity."

"You want taking risks to feel as necessary as eating. (Your favourite thing to eat? The competition. Though you also have a taste for danger.)"

"I'm the expert at turning stealth into wealth."

"Welcome to my Power House. Take a seat, make yourself uncomfortable."

We also leaned on her dance background to increase the uniqueness of the language. Obviously, making moves ties in perfectly with the positioning concept, and we also used messaging like:

"Business success choreography at its finest."

ACTIONS

- Which type of positioning concept are you immediately drawn to? Identity, theme, movement, idea, or style?
- Get creative! What are the different ways you could build out a concept for your brand? Is there one that feels strongest?
- How could this translate to the other areas of your brand?

PHASE 4: EXPAND YOUR IMPACT

Once you've explored your brain, extracted your edge, expressed your truth, and developed your power perspectives, proprietary framework, and positioning concept, it's time to become known for them. Having them is one thing, owning them publicly is another. To actually become the irresistible authority, you need to share your wisdom with the world in ways that feel aligned. As a thought leader with a personal brand in the online space, visibility isn't optional. When you have all the elements of the WisdomBranding framework, showing up and sharing your life's work will feel like a dopamine hit and an exhale of relief at the same time. Your impact depends on your ability to make your vision visible. Your demand depends on your ability to talk about the way you think with conviction. Your results depend on your ability to trust yourself to match delivery with the expectations your brand presence creates. That leads us to the final phase of the framework.

PHASE 4 OF THE WISDOMBRANDING FRAMEWORK: EXPAND YOUR IMPACT

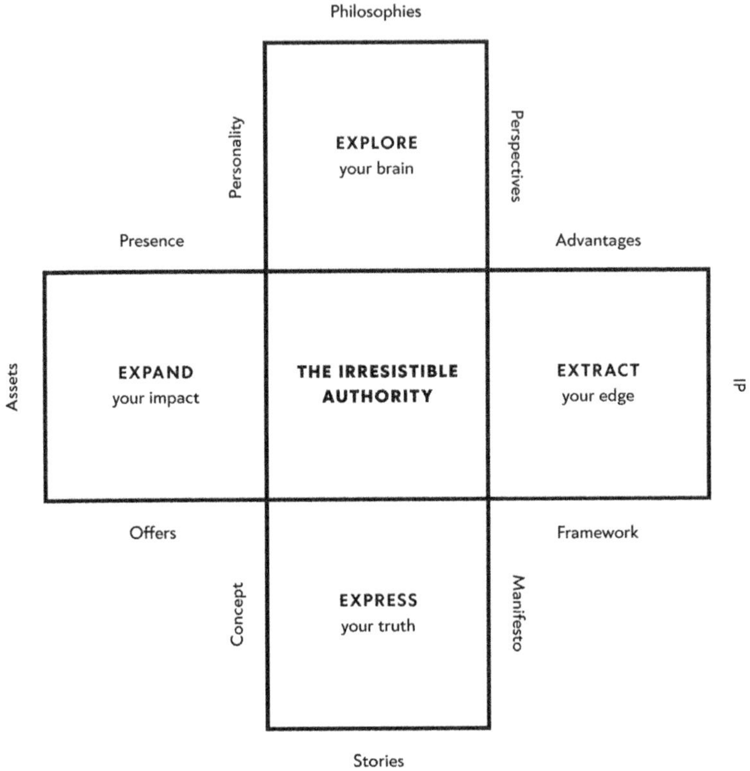

Offers: Develop a deliciously positioned offer suite that allows you to provide a high level of impact in a way that respects your energetic capacity and lifestyle desires.

Assets: Infuse your genius into authority assets (website, podcasts, books, keynotes, etc.) that get you recognised and rewarded on a more significant scale.

Presence: Exude authority in a way that feels good with a powerful and peaceful presence that captivates the right clients and opportunities.

Core phase outcome: presence strategy.

Expanding your impact is more about depth than breadth. Focus on the hearts and minds of those who can most benefit from being in your world. As your impact ripples, stay connected with your core. More eyeballs invite more opinions. Those opinions don't have to change the way you show up. You don't want to do all this work to escape the epidemic of generic only to find yourself back there thanks to well-intentioned advice you didn't ask for from people who aren't brave enough to do what you've done.

14

OFFERS

Your offers are not your brand. They're a piece of the puzzle. When people get knotted about their messaging it's usually because:

- They're not understanding the difference between brand messaging and offer messaging.
- They're lacking clarity in the outcomes their offers provide and the person best positioned to achieve those outcomes.
- They don't know what they stand for and against (or haven't grounded themselves in what they want to stand for and against).
- They have a number of different offers for different people (or it's the same person at different stages of their journey), which makes it difficult to settle on an "umbrella" message.
- They don't know their audience well enough to know what they want.

Disclaimer: I'm not saying do a load of market research and give your audience what they say they want, because 1) you may not want to deliver that, and 2) what people *say* they want is often not what they actually want. It's for you, as the expert, to discern which offer will change your ideal client's life, package and position it accordingly, and articulate the value of it so clearly it practically sells itself.

Power perspectives communicate your unique thoughts on your industry, the way you approach your work and why. Offers are the way you actually deliver the work. They're an extension of your brand. When you started your business, all you needed was an offer and someone to say yes. But as you grow, raise your rates, evolve your ideal client, solidify your processes, try new things, and get better results, you create a brand beyond offers. An offer is how you make money, but your *brand* is how you stimulate demand and desire for your offers. This is the reputation you build through your thought leadership and delivering on your promises. It's why when you *are* an irresistible authority, and your offer has a strong purpose that fulfils an unmet need – it sells with ease.

Offer design is a whole process in itself and depends on so many factors. It's not just whether you have the expertise and experience to solve a specific problem, it's also:

- Does this make sense in the context of your overarching brand positioning and message?
- Do you love to work in this way? If it doesn't light you up, it's not sustainable.
- Does this offer suit your lifestyle? If it demands large amounts of mental or emotional bandwidth, does your expectation fit within the capacity you have?

- Does this offer allow you to reach your goals? Does the maths add up?
- Is this offer scalable? (It doesn't have to be, but worth considering upfront.)
- Can you build an identity and campaign around this offer that is still aligned with your main brand?

THE SEVEN P'S

As a thought leader with something to sell, you need to have offers. What those offers are, specifically, will depend on your personality, capacity, goals, lifestyle desires, and so much more. They could be services, group experiences, courses, or products.

Some people choose to focus on one or two core offers and consider anything else a distraction, while others choose to have tons of offers. There's no right or wrong, though I have my preference! The benefit of having a signature offer (or even a small signature suite of offers) is that you can become known for it. You can develop mastery in delivering that offer. You can build a body of results that make marketing and selling the offer so much easier. You can focus on improving the experience and raise the price in accordance. You can put the majority of your energy into that offer. The downside? You may get bored of delivering the same thing (though don't mistake boredom for the ease that comes with mastery). You may want to work with more than one audience in more than one way, have stackable revenue, and diversify your income streams. Even if this is the case, solidifying one signature offer first will put you in a much stronger position when building out an offer ecosystem.

A problem I often see is that people don't give themselves long enough to position, market, and deliver an offer before deciding to change it, especially if it's something quite different or more evolved from what they've previously sold. It can be so easy to think something isn't working and go back to what feels more familiar than to commit to getting enough data about an offer before making changes.

Wherever you fall, there are seven pieces you need to have in place to ensure you're positioning your offer so the right people see why it's a must-have in their lives, and then have different ways of communicating that information so it buries itself into their brains and instils the certainty required to say yes.

1. Person

The Who. This must be *specific.* Who is this offer perfect for? Your offer needs to be designed for the 3%ers.

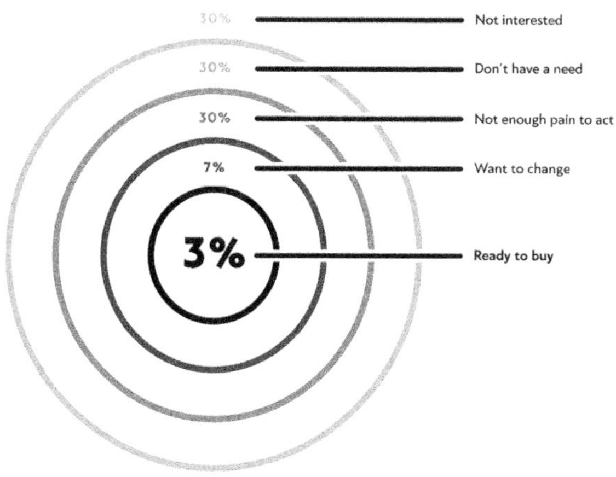

These are the "bullseye" people in your audience who are actively looking for and ready to buy what you're selling and are *already primed* to get the result you offer.

Who are they? What high-level problems do they have? What have they already achieved and overcome? What's happening in their internal and external world that makes them perfect for this offer? What do they *already have in place* that means they are most likely to get the result? What are the prerequisites to being selected? (You're choosing them just as much as they're choosing you.) What drives them? What have they already tried? What fears do they still have and why? What could trip them up? Get granular. It's their psychographics (attitudes, values, desires, habits, interests, lifestyle choices, etc.) that matter more than their demographics (how old they are, where they live, etc.).

Think about the people you've *loved* working with before. What mindset did they have? What kind of personality? What little shifts, actions, and wins did you witness them achieve during your work together that helped them get what they actually came to you for?

2. *Problem*

The Why. This must be *significant*. What is the core problem this offer solves for the person you've specified? Your offer needs to fulfil an unmet need, otherwise there won't be enough motivation to move. This could range from a problem causing them pain to a desire they'll do anything to achieve. This offer needs to take them closer to an ultimate result, even if this particular offer doesn't solve all their problems (which, of course, it won't!).

Two important notes on the "don't use pain points in your marketing" conversation:

1. This doesn't mean potential buyers suddenly don't have problems, but the more sophisticated their awareness gets, the less you need to focus on the problem itself. They're in the market for the solution, and that's what they need selling on. Why you? Why your offer? Saying: "You're so ready to make [desired result] happen!" is not going to cut it.
2. There's a big difference between twisting the knife to make someone feel like crap about their situation and showing that you intimately understand the position a person is in and why they want to experience change from a place of strength (I call the latter empowering empathy). Twisting the knife: "You recoil every time you look in the mirror because your stomach looks like Gollum's buttcheeks." Empowering empathy: "You grew a tiny human in that stomach! And even though it looks different now, you know you have the capacity to love it again. Yep, even with the stretch marks." You're still connecting with the problem a potential buyer wants solved, but in a very different way.

3. Promise

The What. This must be *desirable*. What result are you so confident they will get it's practically inevitable? Why do they want this result now? There needs to be motivation to move now rather than next month or next year. If you're talking to the right person, they will already be in the best position to get this result. We want to make it as easy as possible for this promise to be met when they go through your process. The *transformation* is what people are buying.

The fastest way to lose trust in business is to make a promise you cannot keep. The key is to be confident in your capabilities to deliver but not to *over*promise. This is where boundaries become crucial. If you choose to accept a client who is *not* in the best position to achieve this result, and then they don't achieve the result even though you do everything required on your end, what will you make that mean? It doesn't mean you're not excellent at what you do, or that you're overcharging, or that you need to change your messaging. It means you need to be crystal clear on *who* is the right person for this offer first, speak only to them, and work only with them.

Once we have our core promise, we also want to attach smaller, specific outcomes that collectively achieve that promise. Note that the promise does not have to be fulfilled by the time the offer is complete. High-level results are rarely immediate. You don't need to dilute your promise, just make sure your client is properly equipped to achieve that promise even once your time together is finished.

4. Process

The How. This must be *different*. How do you facilitate the result you promise? How is that different from what your person may have already tried? How is it different from the other solutions available to them? This is where we get to introduce our unique frameworks, skills, tools, modalities, methods, etc.

What are the tiny transformations your best-fit client will experience when working with you through this process? What are those 1% improvements they will experience that when compounded, will help them reach the result they want? Think of these like breadcrumbs that are sprinkled along the path you're walking together, that lead them to the outcome you promise. Looking at the tiny transformations can help you get more specific about how you actually help your dream clients. While you want to be clear about the core promise you offer, it can be difficult for a prospect to see how it's possible, *even if* they're a perfect fit. If it feels too far away or seems too good to be true, tiny transformations help bridge the gap. For example, let's say your promise is: *"Lose the weight you gained during pregnancy in a way that's kind to your mind and easy to fit into life with a little one."* A tiny transformation could be: *"You're actually excited to eat spinach thanks to the secret smoothie recipe all my clients love so much it's permanently replaced their sweet afternoon snack."*

5. *Possibilities*

If the right person with the right problem goes through this process and achieves the result you promise, what becomes possible for them? Who are they now? How do they see themselves? How do they feel? What doors can they open that they couldn't before? This is about painting a picture for people of what is a very real possibility for them once their need is met.

There's a big difference between making wild promises to potential clients in order to win the yes and showing the scope of possibilities of working with you and what it truly requires from both sides to reach those results. Many of the clients I work with are so repelled at the thought of doing the first that they don't lean far enough into doing the second, and that's why it's harder for their dream clients to understand the potential transformation available to them, and the likelihood of them achieving it with support. Lean in. Showing the possibility is not the same as making promises you can't keep.

6. Power Perspectives

What will make your person pay attention to this offer? What will hook them, or act as a pattern interrupt for them? Alongside your core brand power perspectives, your offers can have their own individual power perspectives. This is where much of the contextual offer messaging will come from.

7. Package

How can you package this offer in a captivating way? Your offers are like mini brands. They all fall under your main brand but have an identity of their own. Think of it like individual albums from the same musical artist. Brand the offer by giving it a unique name, conceptual direction, price, and (if necessary) visuals.

In 2023, I created a pop-up offer called Hooked. It was an impulsive idea that came to me as I was brushing my teeth, driven by the perspectives I had around AI at the time, and here's a summary of how the *Seven Ps* broke down for it.

Person: The deliberate yet daring online business owner (I could definitely have been more specific here!).

Problem: Wants to hook their audience in fresh ways without using AI or creating more content that contributes to the noise online.

Promise: An entire year's worth of storymarketing hooks mapped for you in a day.

Process: Spend the day together going back and forth on Voxer. I'll interrogate you and turn the brilliance in your brain into fifty hooks that will be delivered to you in a Google Doc.

Possibilities: Grow your ideal audience and become more of an authority through your body of work.

Power Perspective: You don't have to be the loudest in the room, but you do have to be one of the most intriguing.

Package: Hooked, intro price of £1250, no visuals (as this was a test version).

I was inundated with enquiries and oversold the spaces available for this offer to absolute dream clients by sending just one email to a small list of under 1000 people, which I also duplicated on my Facebook profile.

Once you're clear on your *Seven Ps*, get that offer out into the world! As you work with more people, you can evolve the Ps so your offer is always clearly positioned for the person you want to work with *most*. And if you get the itch to scrap an excellent offer, consider whether you can scratch that itch by being more creative in your *marketing* versus creating a whole new offer.

ACTIONS

- Decide which offer you want to focus on selling next (existing or new).
- Take it through the Seven Ps process.

15

ASSETS

What comes to mind when you think about authority? Perhaps it's something like:

- Power
- Hierarchy
- Pedestals
- Smart
- Rules
- Uniform
- Obedience
- Leadership
- Confidence
- Knowledge

I'd argue that many of these have a masculine vibe, which could make you feel like showing up as an authority means leaning more heavily into your masculine, especially if you're a woman who has been programmed to believe that in order to get where you want to in life you need to "act more like a man". Show your strengths, hide your vulnerability. If you show that you're flawed, that you're *human*, you risk rocking the pedestal you never asked to be put on. It's why so much content we see is "how-to" focused. By homing in on the practical part, we can skip the emotional part, even though we know it's *emotions* that make people buy. You have to move someone emotionally before you can move someone physically. I'd argue this isn't authority content at all. Is it valuable? Maybe. Does it show me you know what you're talking about? Probably. Am I drawn to you as a result of that? Hmm, I'm going to need to see some deeper layers. That's where the irresistible part comes in.

As a personal brand, your vehicle to becoming an irresistible authority is thought leadership – sharing your power perspectives in a way that means the right people can understand and trust you're the perfect person to help solve a problem or fulfil a desire they have. Any kind of leadership, *strong* leadership, requires vulnerability. It's being witnessed in our humanness and finding connection in our compassion that makes us irresistible. Does that mean showing up as a hot mess? No – though you could probably brand that if you really wanted to! I'm sure it would be relatable. But we're not necessarily going for relatable. We're going for relevant and resonant. When you know what you want to say, you've got to have places to share it. That's where authority assets come in.

CHOOSING YOUR ASSETS

Authority assets are the physical manifestations of your intellectual property. As a reminder, IP is anything you create with your mind. It includes:

- Power perspectives
- Frameworks
- Teaching concepts / tools
- Names of products, programs, and services
- Content / copy
- Teaching concepts
- Trademarks
- Methods / systems

Assets are things like:

- Website
- Blog
- Curriculum for courses / programs
- Certification
- Digital products
- Podcast
- Emails
- Social media posts
- Book
- Keynotes / presentations

Authority assets are intentionally infused with your IP. They're distinctive to your brand. You own them. They form a huge part of your online presence and support you in becoming known and recognised as an authority. They are the *vehicles* for your wisdom. Remember, your brain is your biggest asset, but the way we experience your brain is through your physical creations. Authority assets are places where your intellectual property lives and breathes. You get to choose which authority assets you create. See them as an ecosystem – everything supports everything. The assets might be separate, but they live under one roof. Just like stories, this is how you can share the same message in different ways, based both on how you like to create and how your audience likes to consume.

When it comes to your IP and authority assets, you're building a *body of work*. A collection of your ideas. The result of which compounds with patience. You can't make a tree grow just by willing it to. It's the compound effect of time, water, and sunshine that makes that happen. Focus less on the speed of the impact and more on the environment that creates it. You can't tell your whole life story in five minutes, and it's the same for your perspectives in your authority assets.

The compound effect can also work the other way. If you keep your ideas locked inside you, what impact can they really make? The longer you keep your wisdom a secret, the harder it can become to share it. That's why I suggest you choose your authority assets wisely. Just because *they* have a podcast doesn't mean you have to. I do recommend every personal brand has a proper website, though, one that show-cases your power perspectives, proprietary framework, and positioning concept. It's an immediate trust trigger. Some people will tell you they've built a brand without one, and while that may be true for them, a website can do *so much* heavy lifting for you before you even get to other forms of communication. I'd much rather a person booked or bought directly through my website than have to go through a lengthy direct message exchange for them to get the details they need to make a decision.

- How do your clients generally find you?

- If you knew 100 new, perfect-fit people would enter your world tomorrow, how would like them to have got there?
- What are your goals beyond working with clients? Writing a book? Speaking on stages? Developing a certification?
- What kind of authority assets are most likely to help you reach those goals?
- What is your strongest form of communication? How could you leverage this more? e.g., if you're comfortable being on video, could you focus on a YouTube channel?
- What have you been dreaming about creating for ages but haven't done yet?
- Is there an unconventional asset you could create? For example, in late 2020/early 2021 I created what I called a secret podcast, before private podcasts became popular. This allowed me to express my perspectives in a new way, with the safety of it being "behind closed doors" and it got great feedback. (The only reason I stopped was because I got pregnant, and the fatigue wiped me out!)

ACTIONS

- Update your website in line with your power perspectives, proprietary framework, and positioning concept.
- Choose your priority authority asset.
- Consider which other authority assets would best support your body of work.

16

PRESENCE

Your job is to focus on what you *can* control and surrender to what you can't. You can control your presence – where and how you show up – but you can't control the result of it. I've never in my life been fishing but let's imagine me in waders for a moment with a massive rod in my hands. I can control:

- Where I fish.
- The bait I put on the rod.
- The rod itself.
- Where I throw my line (to a degree).
- How long I wait.

I can get all of the above perfect according to fishing wisdom, and I still can't control what I catch. Then it's a matter of patience, persistence, and making adjustments based on intuition and data. Your online presence is the same. There are a number of things you can control, and you can give yourself the best possible chance of getting the results you want but attaching yourself so much to an outcome that hasn't materialised yet is exactly what will take your focus away from what *will* create that outcome. Business owners can tie themselves in knots when they spend too much time focusing on the uncontrollable rather than what's in their control:

- Where they have a presence (e.g., website, social media, in person).
- The "bait" they use (I mean this in a neutral sense, this is just another way of saying content of any kind).
- Their energy and appearance.
- Where they put their focus (e.g., short-form video, long-form blogs, in-person networking events).
- How long they spend there.

There's a reason I focus on presence here rather than marketing. Your marketing strategy is a plan for how you get yourself in front of the people who need your offers, but if that involves having a presence in places that you don't like, that doesn't feel good to your nervous system and that doesn't play to your strengths, you're never going to show up as your most captivating self. Just because big brands have omnipresence doesn't mean you need it. You're not selling to the masses, but you do need to be visible to more of the right people. The truth is, any marketing strategy can work. People have success in so many different ways and you have more choice than you think.

What kind of presence do you want? What feels like a full-body *yes*? What feels like a full-body *no*? How do you want others to feel in your presence? Is the way you're showing up aligned with all of those? I want a peaceful and powerful presence. Peaceful means feeling calm, grounded, and comfortable in my expression. Powerful means being strong, convicted, and bold in my expression. What is the opposite of this?

- Having to show up at predefined times.
- Having to show up every day.
- Creating noisy, fluffy content.
- Doing lots of videos.
- Delivering regular live content.
- Spending a significant amount of time on social media apps.

You can become more visible while still feeling comfortable. If you want to take up more space, and you absolutely should, it better be a space you enjoy being in. Decide what an intentional presence looks like for you and choose your marketing activities from there. I can't count the number of times my clients have poured hours into having a consistent Instagram presence and then told me that's not where they get their clients! Then they doubled down on their presence elsewhere and saw an immediate improvement in results. That doesn't mean they shouldn't have an Instagram presence if they want one, but it might not be where they choose to put the most energy.

THE CURSE OF THE PERSONAL BRAND

My husband and I mini-mooned at a gorgeous country hotel called The Fish and as you might expect, they had an array of seafood on their dinner menu. The restaurant was stunning, and as we tucked into our tongue-tingling starters, we decided to play a game – look around and take a sip for every person you see on their phone. It's not a particularly fun game to be honest, especially when you're pregnant and can't do it with Malbec. It always surprises and saddens me to see how many people who have chosen to meet in person in a beautiful place have also chosen to give so much of their attention to a tiny screen.

This is one of the curses of the online personal brand. On the upside, everything is a content opportunity. On the downside, everything is a content opportunity. Rather than revel in the present moment, there's an industry pressure to make sure you document the moment to show other people. It's like going to a live concert and recording the whole thing on your phone. Why? You're robbing yourself of the real, in-the-now, human experience. Think about it. How many people do you follow whose Instagram stories never run out? This isn't an issue if a person genuinely loves and lives for sharing constantly (though I would question how healthy and sustainable that is). Some people also have teams who handle this presence for them full-time, but the majority of small, online business owners don't.

If I had a pound for every time I've heard the phrase *"just be consistent"* I would be considerably richer than I am now. Yes, consistency can help develop an online presence – I'm not saying it's not important, but not if what you're sharing is irrelevant. It doesn't matter if you post consistently – whether that's every day, a few times a week, or once a month – if it doesn't captivate people. And you have to captivate before you convert. That's why I believe in focusing on potency over consistency. You don't become memorable just because you show up on a regular basis. You become memorable because you create tiny transformations within people. Consistency means nothing if you're sharing the wrong message.

You're an intellectual artist. Artists don't put pressure on themselves to create masterpieces every day. You don't want to share "content" for the sake of sharing; that's just contributing to the noise. Many people do this and it's why they find marketing so draining. Instead, rise above the noise by playing on a whole different frequency. You don't need to have the loudest voice to become the strongest presence. Share perspectives that intrigue people. Share stories that move people, that make them want to read the next one, that stay with them long after they've read them. Create an online presence where it's less, "Look at me!" and more, "I'm going to make your world a better place by being present in it." That's when tiny transformations compound to become big ones.

PIECING TOGETHER A STRATEGY

When you know how you want your presence to feel, then you can bring some strategy to the table. This will all depend on your personality, capacity, and (to a degree) your desired audience.

Website

As mentioned, I strongly recommend having a website as a personal brand, especially for SEO purposes. This works for you 24/7 and should form the centre of your presence ecosystem. If there's one place you go all out, make it your website! Be the most captivating version of yourself there.

Platform

Which place feels like the sweet spot between where you love to hang out and how your audience loves to consume content? What leverages your strengths in the best way? If you could only share your power perspectives in one place, where would you choose? Use the platform that already feels most natural to you and double down on building your authority there before worrying about stacking and achieving omnipresence. Don't make assumptions about where "the right people" may or may not be. For example, Jade Tambini (B2B Jade) who I mentioned earlier works with marketers with significant budgets in small and medium-sized enterprises. The automatic response might be that her audience is on LinkedIn. And they probably are. But she focuses her presence predominantly on TikTok. She enjoys showing up there, and she's developed an incredible reputation as a result.

Audience

Think about the person who is the best fit for your most profitable offer and focus on them in your communications. Focus on the audience you *already have* and get clearer and more accurate with how you talk to the potential clients who are already in your presence before considering how to find a whole other pool of people. The right people are everywhere, it's a case of speaking directly to them. Having a small audience is not an issue if what you have to share with them is relevant and resonant.

Cadence

I've spoken about how potency is more important than consistency. While I don't believe you need strict schedules, it can help to set a cadence for your presence. This is like a rhythm for the way you like to show up. Do you prefer to batch and drip content? Are you creating space for that? Do you prefer to create off the cuff? Would having a light structure actually support your creative impulse? All that being said, trust that whatever you want to share, whenever and wherever, is exactly what the right people need to hear. Take the pressure off whether this "fits" within your brand or schedule, and allow your perspectives to meet the public.

Energy

Energy can be felt. You can have the most gorgeous website in the world, but it won't do its job if you don't fully stand behind your messaging. Likewise, if your energy is strong, you can sell with a simple Google Doc. When do you feel your most powerful self? Irresistible authorities don't have to be present all the time because their presence is felt long after they've left the room. Remember, you're intentionally becoming a person of interest, and you can be different versions of yourself depending on where you are. For example, you could create serious thought pieces for LinkedIn and then be causal on Instagram Stories. The energy and the way you share how you think will be different, but it's still congruent with who you are.

Collaborations

One of the fastest ways to expand your impact is to leverage *other people's* presence. The authority assets you use as a vehicle for your voice don't have to be your own. Consider being a resident/guest expert in paid containers, featuring on podcasts, doing joint ventures, PR, etc. Whose audience would get value from your viewpoints? It's crucial to be clear on your power perspectives beforehand, to maximise the impact you make.

Repurposing

What can you repurpose from your existing body of work? Can you build repurposing into your presence strategy, perhaps with the help of AI? Effective repurposing can be the simplest and quickest way to have a presence in more places without piling more creation onto your plate.

THE COURAGE ZONE

You don't have to leave your comfort zone entirely for magical things to happen. We've all heard the phrase: *"The magic happens outside your comfort zone."* That can sound thrilling to people addicted to adrenaline but awful to those who would prefer not to fry their nervous system in an online microwave. You don't need to leave your comfort zone; you can find your courage zone. This lives on the edge of your comfort zone. It's a place that brings a sense of safety but is a portal to growth. Being there stretches you in new ways and then stretches your comfort zone. Once you know you can make it through something once, you're automatically more confident you can make it through it again.

Being in the epidemic of generic is like being in your comfort zone but finding it a bit uncomfortable. Which makes no sense to a logical mind. It's like staying in a relationship because it's familiar rather than leaving to pursue the love of your life. The longer you stay where you are, the more uncomfortable you'll become. Until it isn't a comfort zone at all. You're showing up and sharing things that remind you of comfort rather than emboldening yourself and saying what you really want to say. However uncomfortable the idea of expressing your truth is pales in comparison to how uncomfortable you'll feel keeping it locked up inside you. Stop sitting on your goldmine and start sharing it. Your voice matters. Your presence is needed. Your leadership will change lives. Find your courage zone and you'll find your power, your peace, and your people.

ACTIONS

- Create your feel-good presence strategy.
- Consider what moves you could make from your courage zone.

17

THE CRISP COMMUNICATION FRAMEWORK

Branding is the art of captivation. But how do you move someone from being captivated (paying with their attention) to converted (paying with their money)? As I mentioned earlier in this book, you've heard that people need to "know, like, and trust" you, but the kind of certainty required to buy – particularly for higher ticket offers – goes far deeper than that. There are many people I know, like, and trust, but don't buy from. Instead, focus on moving people up the ladder of certainty. There are three rungs to climb. Certainty in you, certainty in your offer, and certainty in themselves. This isn't about convincing people to do anything they don't want to, it's about shaping a narrative that shows people why you're the right choice, the best choice, and ultimately, the only choice.

1. Certainty in You

If someone is going to pay you hundreds or thousands of their well-earned money, they must feel certain about you. They must believe that what you say is true, that you're a person of integrity who will do what you say, and that what they see before they buy is the same as what they'll get after they buy. People want to know that you're not just an excellent marketer, but an excellent deliverer. If *you're* not certain in all of the above, they won't be either.

2. Certainty in Your Offer

They must believe that *this* offer is going to get them the result they want. When you're clear on your *Seven Ps,* it will be significantly easier to build this belief. You can boost this by providing social proof, showing how and *why* your process works, and the ways this offer has been deliberately designed to be the best fit.

3. Certainty in Themselves

A person can feel certain in you and your offer and still not say yes to it. That's because they're lacking certainty that *they* will get the result you promise. This is another reason why it's so important your offers speak to those who are already at an advanced level of readiness and trust in their own abilities to do what is necessary. Your brand and communications don't exist to *convince* someone of what's possible. They exist to *affirm* what they subconsciously already know is possible.

How do we move people up these three rungs of certainty? Energetic transfer and clear communication. I'm going to show you how to do both of these using my proprietary CRISP Communication Framework, a simple and forever-effective framework for creating relevant and resonant content on any platform.

C: Challenge
R: Root
I: Invested
S: Solution
P: Possibility

Challenge

What is the challenge, problem, or unfulfilled desire your best-fit person is experiencing right now? Make sure it's specific and accurate. Join the conversation happening in their head. What they are saying to themselves is unlikely to be what they would say out loud (another reason why market research and swiping the language people use isn't always the best approach). There has to be some jeopardy involved here. The challenge has to be significant enough that a person is driven to overcome it. What would happen if they didn't? What's at risk? This doesn't have to be a tangible risk; it could be an identity one. We hear of the importance of ROI (return on investment), but there's always a potential COI (cost of inaction) too.

Root

What's the root cause of this challenge and the consequences of it? How can you bring awareness to the *real* reason for the issue? This could be related to identity, beliefs, circumstances, knowledge/skills gaps, or actions (or lack of). This is where you can start to show your power perspectives and original insights. Note that what *they* think the root cause is may not actually be the root cause. What lies are they telling themselves about why they're in this position? Remember, you're crafting the narrative to show that *you* are the right person to help. In reality, multiple solutions could be suitable, it all depends on how you frame the root.

A great way to uncover the root cause of a problem is to go through the *Five Whys*. This is a Lean Six Sigma tool that can be transferred here, though you may not need five to get to your root! Let's look at two different ways you could approach the same challenge. I'm keeping this example super simple. First, let's imagine you're a positioning and messaging expert.

Challenge: I don't have enough qualified leads coming into the business.

Why: I'm not sure who the right audience is.
Why: I haven't tested enough messaging.
Why: I struggle to find compelling words that stand out.
Why: I don't know what makes me different.

They may *think* the issue is that they don't know their audience, but you can help them see the real issue is positioning. Then you can present a relevant solution. Let's take the same example, but this time, you're a YouTube video strategist.

Challenge: I don't have enough qualified leads coming into the business.

Why: I'm not visible enough.
Why: I hate doing reels.
Why: It takes so long, and I rarely get enquiries anyway.

They may *think* the issue is lack of visibility, but you can help them see that the real issue is that they're using the wrong kind of video and they're on the wrong platform. Then you can present a relevant solution.

Do you see how you can craft your narrative based on the way you approach this exercise? The key is making sure that you know your solution to be a real one!

Invested

Where have they already invested time, money, energy, or other resources to try to overcome their challenge? Why hasn't it worked for them (yet)? Be sure to empathise here so they know it's not because there's something "wrong" with them. Remember, you always want to be speaking to empowered, motivated people who are in the best position to get the result you offer. What fears remain for them that could get in the way?

Solution

What do you know to be the true solution to their problem? How do you know? Why will this work? Who do they need to be and what do they need to already have to give them the best chance of getting this result? You want your solution to address people's fears and help show how you can close the gap. This is also where you can show your power perspectives around your area of expertise, highlight your advantages, and share your framework.

Possibility

What's possible when they have overcome their challenge? What is available to them from that place? What are the natural, potential consequences of your solution? How do you know? This is not about making promises or guarantees, it's about painting the possibility with nuance and context.

Here's a very simple example I've used this framework to create.

Challenge

You've worked so hard to increase your visibility, and it's brought you a handful of clients who've given you blush-worthy testimonials, but you feel like you're constantly creating content and your message is getting lost amongst the noise online. You've proven you can get the right people results, but you're not being noticed by enough of them.

Root

Here's the real reason this is happening. You're watering down your message, so instead of saying what your people need to hear to hire you, you're saying everything they've already heard from your competitors. *That's* why your message isn't getting traction.

Invested

I know you've created more content in the hope it will please the algorithm. But creating more of what's already diluted is only going to keep you on the exhausting content hamster wheel.

Solution

Instead, you need to increase the *potency* of your message. That way, you create a huge emotional impact with *fewer* pieces of content and have dream clients landing in your inbox saying, *"How can I work with you?"* This is exactly what I help my clients do.

Possibility

When you're calling in *more* dream clients by creating *less* content, you have extra space to write your book, take long lunchtime walks, and, of course, deliver an out-of-this-world result to your client that will have them referring you all over the internet.

18

A FINAL NOTE FROM ME

Captivation isn't a fluke, it's an art. When you see your brain as a liquid goldmine, your brand can become a literal one. The unique combination of your power perspectives, proprietary framework, positioning concept, and presence strategy is everything you need to become the irresistible authority and make the competition irrelevant. A whole new world of opportunities is about to become available to you, and you're ready to claim them.

WisdomBranding is branding the way you think – and the way you think is exactly what the world needs. It's about leading yourself with love and courage and using the wisdom within to show up in ways that serve both you and the people you dream of working with. A brand is merely a perception, and when you lean into that, you realise you have significant control in shaping that perception. You can be one of many service providers, creatives, coaches, or consultants, or you can be The One.

The One stands in a league of their own. They're a thought leader who brings fresh perspectives to the table they're building as they go. The table is made of evidence, faith, and fine mahogany. They're an intellectual pioneer who creates tiny transformations in people at every touchpoint, not because they're engineering a sale, but because it's at the core of who they are. They're change makers and rule breakers. They know what makes them unique and they're smart enough to use it to their advantage. They trust that who they are right now is enough. *They are you.*

I hope you've enjoyed reading this book, but more so, I hope you've enjoyed exploring what your brand could become. You're a masterpiece in the making. If you'd like my help to monetise your mind and become the must-have in your market, email me directly at **suzi@captivationhouse.com** or come find me at **www.captivationhouse.com**. *I think we'd make a stellar team.*

ABOUT THE AUTHOR

Suzi Gray is a brand positioning and messaging expert and the founder of Captivation House. She's a thought partner and consultant to established online business owners who want to brand the way they think and become the must-have in their market. She lives on a marina just outside Cardiff, UK, with her husband and son.

Printed in Great Britain
by Amazon

40294976R00119